Praise for CAT SKILLS: *Loving Care for Cats*

"Cat Skills had me laughing from page one! But mostly, I was nodding in agreement. It is incredibly well-researched but not at all dull like so many pet care books. (The section on nutrition and what to look for on cat food labels alone is invaluable.) Whether you are a lifelong cat owner like me or experiencing the joy of being owned by a feline for the very first time, I guarantee you will enjoy this book. **Lisa Richman, A Tonk's Tale.com**

"Written in a conversational style and infused with fun cat quotes and illustrations. Did you know that there are certain words ("passwords") that most cats will respond to? Every cat deserves the best life possible and this book gives cat lovers tons of extra tips and tricks to help make that happen!" **Melissa LaPierre, Mochas, Mysteries and Meows.com**

"I loved this book! I bought Cat Skills because I had a few kitty problems. I've had lots of cats, so I thought, what can I learn from a cat book? I was hooked from page one and read through the whole book, cover to cover in three days. I never do that. There are so many helpful ideas in this book that I had never heard before. She writes in a very entertaining way. I was skeptical when I read that there was a certain way to call your cats to get their attention. Then I tried it and all three cats came running into the room! A must have for new cat caretakers as well as diehard cat people."--**Brenda Hart, Forgotten Felines Rescue**

Photo©Kerri Lee Smith

ISBN-13: 978-0692305706

Esperanza Press

**Dedicated to every cat looking for a home
and in memory of our lost loves; the victims of F.I.P.**

Disclaimer: *The information herein is not intended to replace professional advice from your own veterinarian and nothing herein is intended as a medical diagnosis or treatment. Any questions about your animal's health should be directed to your veterinarian.*

*Front cover art "Little Enid in Red Chair" © Harry Boardman
Photo on back cover courtesy of Wikihow.com*

Contents

Acknowledgements

I thank Wendy King, Karen Grohs, Cynthia Brooks, Marsha Forsyth, Richard Kibbsgaard, Gina Zaro, and all the other cat lovers who shared their cat skills. Your cat buddies are lucky to own you! Molto Grazie a Viola and to everyone who allowed me to use their photos including Magnus Brath, J.D. Crowe, Sue Fockner, John Ginn, Ana Helston, Katie Procyk, Jason Thorpe, Joanne Wegiel, Jenna Workman, Tommy Hemmert-Olesen, Kate Tomlinson, Kerri Lee Smith and Wikihow.com.

Special thanks to Leah Hanley, DVM, Jean Hofve, DVM, Tanya Traufield and Jenna Rogers of the Longmont, CO Humane Society, Jody Donohue and Laurie Miller.

I am very grateful to Kathy Dieterich and Janis Rapoport de Miranda for reading, for editing and for their support.

Photo©Jason Thorpe

Introduction

Whether you've just adopted your first kitten or you want to add to your cat skills, here are secrets to living happily ever with a cat. Learn to speak fluent Feline, including the one special password that will make your cat sit up and take notice every time.

Tips from the pros on care and feeding: Cat lovers, animal shelter experts and veterinarians all share their wisdom to keep your cat buddies happy and healthy. This book is the result of hundreds of hours of research and product testing to offer a comprehensive guide to the latest in cat care, cat feeding and cat health...even helping senior cats live longer and coping with grief and loss.

There are simple solutions for problem behaviors.
End litter box boycotting, destructive scratching and get
help integrating new cats into your family. Tips for raising
kittens and solutions to many more common problems will
make living with your cats a joy. You'll even find money-
saving tips that will pay for this book twice over.

Anyone can learn easy and gentle ways of modifying cat
behavior, and master the secret language of cats.

Cat skills for mere mortals include voice training, trimming
toenails, giving pills and brushing teeth.

Photo©Leslie Goodwin

Bonus sections: TOXINS/POISONS/DANGERS, FAQs and
CATALOG of internet sites at the end.

Photo©Kerri Lee Smith

WHAT MAKES THEM TICK?

Living wild, cats are elegantly self-sufficient. Felines are expert escape artists who can run thirty miles an hour then run thirty feet straight up a tree. They tread lightly and raise their litters mostly unseen and unheard by their many predators.

Cats are skilled, efficient hunters, but despite needle like claws and trigger reflexes, they must sleep with one eye open. There are more than six other mammals and even some birds who hunt them and kidnap their kittens.

WHAT MAKES THEM TICK? continued

Other felines can be a threat, too. Toms wage war against each other, competing for mates and turf.

To stake their territory, they have an ingenious system of marking home fields with smells detectable to all other cats. They can leave scented graffiti with their paws and the glands on their cheeks to warn other cats.

Cats are famously curious; they had to be curious to find dinner. They prefer to hunt alone but will stand together as a colony against a predator. Cats thrive on routine to relieve stress in the struggle to survive. They constantly groom so predators can't track them by smell and cover their wastes for the same reason. Mom cat will move her kittens if the nest is threatened by clutching them by the scruff of the neck. She brings them live prey to teach them to hunt so they also become self-sufficient.

Felines need a safe, secluded hangout where they can relax and hide from predators.

Inside every domestic house cat beats a wild heart, guided by primal instincts and a strong will to survive.

When a pregnant barn cat strayed into my life, she taught me how to raise cat kids. Mom cat, Lucy, was the benevolent dictator of her six kittens. When she carried them, they went limp. When she chirped, they followed. When she howled to announce she had prey, they came running. She always made eye contact with them before "speaking." They often greeted her by touching noses or mouths. When she wanted to be left alone, she hissed in their faces or swatted them with a paw. They never acted rejected. They loved her no less because she hissed, and they instantly obeyed.

A pet cat can stay forever a kitten because we meet his needs. He doesn't have to fend for himself. He can bond to us as he bonded to Mom. *He can allow us to dominate him in the same loving way.*

A cat will be aloof and independent...*if he has to be.*

People who say: "Cats prefer to fend for themselves. They're not affectionate and you can't train them," have never learned the secrets to bonding with a cat. *Cats can learn and they can love. Cats need us as much as we need them!*

Photo©Magnus Brath, www.sunseteo.com

Cats become dependent on us when we understand their needs and meet them. They give and respond to affection when they learn they can trust us...that our kindness is constant. They can even learn how to please us if we clearly communicate our expectations. Cats learn to show love by being loved.

We should be codependent in the best possible way. Cat rescuer, Wendy King, beautifully describes this relationship as *symbiotic.* A bond with a cat can be as deep and fulfilling as any other relationship built on mutual dependence. These "kids" stay children their whole lives. And your cats cost less to send to college! Unlike many relationships, a bond with a cat will get stronger with time.

I offer the following techniques, not knowing your cat and his or her unique personality. Some cats are a mystery wrapped in a riddle inside an enigma.

WHAT MAKES THEM TICK? continued

Some come to us emotionally damaged or were never socialized. They will take longer to bond or to develop trust. Adult cats who never interacted with humans as kittens, who were raised in cages and weaned too young will be slower to respond. Orphaned or bottle-fed kittens may remain fearful for life.

Feral cats are, by definition, wild, and have highly developed self-protective instincts. Some can be tamed with time and patience- especially young ones. I believe that most every cat eventually will respond to proper, consistent treatment that respects their primal instincts.

Le chien est un idiot

The dog is an idiot.

Cats have a public relations problem. Cats are underdogs of the pet world, constantly being negatively compared to dogs. They aren't dogs. They have a totally different psychology. Naturally we should treat them differently.

I have a theory. Cats are French and Dogs are American.

Compare the stereotypes:

THE FRENCH

Socially discriminating

Highly developed palates

**Take long vacations/
Short work week**

**Enjoy paté, eat snails and
frog legs**

Love high fashion

Ethnocentric

CATS

Aloof

Finicky

Sleep 16 hours a day

**Love liver, eat rodents,
chase frogs**

**Groom themselves
constantly**

**Always scent-marking their
space**

AMERICANS

Open and outgoing

Monolingual

Eat lots of junk food

Drink white Zinfandel

Hard working

Overly friendly

DOGS

Love anyone holding a ball

Bark to get their way

Eat out of the garbage

Drink out of the toilet

Do tricks for a biscuit

Sniff crotches

Photo©Jenna Workman

Cat Phobias

To understand a cat's quirky behavior, consider the *short list* of phobias that might cause him to act out:

Being left alone: *We're out of cookies and I need a neck massage!*

Boarding kennels: *Why have I been evicted and what have you done with my family?*

Bullies, human or animal: *The dog stole my dinner and the kids jerked my tail.*

Illness and treatments: *Despite my brave outward appearance, I'm totally freaking out.*

Moving: *I saw a monster under the bed.*

New cat, animal, or person at home: *Why do you like the new baby better than me?*

Redecorating: *How could you give my favorite scratching chair to Goodwill?*

Outdoor cats have all this, plus: predators, neighbor cats, thunder, lightning, heavy rain, fireworks...and the sneakiest killers of all: motor vehicles.

The long list of cat stressors includes almost every other life experience except sleeping and eating in the usual location. Considering their innate fears and phobias, it's no wonder cats sometimes act insecure and neurotic.

They have ways of communicating their distress that often mystify and annoy us but it's never personal. They're bound by instincts. Their quirks make perfect sense.

Most problem behaviors in cats are caused by stress.

Photo ©Jenna Workman

How Cats Cope With Stress

Avoid the litter box...especially if a bully cat is guarding the box to keep him away. More on litter box drama to come in the TROUBLESHOOTING section.

Spray on walls and doors. Spraying can be hormonal or territorial. Even neutered males will spray to mark territory.

How Cats Cope With Stress continued

Some female cats will spray or puddle as well. Female cats in heat will draw suitors who spray mark. Check out the CATALOG at the end for a guide to low-cost spay and neuter clinics in your area.

> *In my house lives a cat who is a curmudgeon and cantankerous, a cat who is charming and convivial. A cat who is combative and commendable. And yet I have but one cat.* **David Edwards**

Scratch surfaces or groom themselves excessively.

Attack. A frightened cat may attack another to assert dominance. A female in heat may attack because of raging hormones. A cat who has been abused may attack to defend himself. A declawed cat may bite because he can no longer use claws to defend himself.

Hide or Withdraw. When he's afraid, a cat reverts to his most primitive instincts to protect himself from harm.

Photo©Leslie Goodwin

Happy Cat Hangouts

To make your home a cool cat hangout, give him places to jump, play, climb and hide.

Each cat needs his own litter box (more on litter boxes to come) in a semi-private place with free access and no bullies keeping him from it, a regular fresh water supply, scratching posts and pads, toys and perches.

He needs his own bed. He's a professional napper and needs the proper workplace for snoozing. Some prefer to be up high and others like to hole up in a quiet corner or under furniture. A wicker basket lined with a pillow makes a purrfect bed.

He needs a safe place to hide if another animal or person is aggressive toward him.

A perch at least three feet above the floor will keep him happy and secure. A ledge in front of a window with fresh air and a view will keep an indoor cat entertained. Some clever cat lovers build cat superhighways throughout the house with ramps, shelves, climbing poles and condos.

Happy Hangouts continued

Your cat will love it if you clear off the top of a book shelf, a windowsill or open the top drawer of a dresser where he can lurk. This will ensure that your clothing will have cat hair pre-installed!

He likes to snack several times a day.

He loves routine...to nap at the same time each day, in his favorite napping spots, to eat at regular times, to go out at regular times. And to keep living in the same house with no newcomers or abrupt changes.

Cats don't smoke. That includes cigarettes and especially Marijuana.

According to the ASPCA, Marijuana is poisonous to cats and dogs whether they eat the plant or inhale the smoke. Dogs who consume marijuana plants or edibles have died from it. Any animal who consumes the plant or breathes the smoke has been poisoned and should see a veterinarian.

Cats and dogs shouldn't be inhaling second hand cigarette smoke either. It can cause asthma or cancer. Not to mention what it does to humans! If you want to keep your animals safe, don't smoke any kind of stogies around them, and especially not wacky tobacky.

New synthetic carpet can emit fumes harmful to cats.

Cats and children can hang themselves in curtain cords. Hanging strings are extremely tempting to kitties, so tie cords out of reach of all the kids. Remember, little paws can get stuck between door and door jamb. *For full list see TOXINS/POISONS/DANGERS section at the end.*

Photo©Joanne Wegiel, thecathouseinc.com

HOW TO MAKE A LOVE BOND

To bond with a cat, he first needs to know he can depend on you and he *must* depend on you for all that is good in life.

If you want a cat to worship you, don't give free access through a cat door. If you open the door to the outdoors or Catio, going out or coming in, your cat learns he must depend on you and needs *to ask you for help.*

You won't just feed him free choice. You will make a point of feeding him. You give great neck massages. You dangle the play birdies. You toss him a treat so he feels special. You're the one who consistently meets his needs and lavishes him with approval and affection. You give him a stable, safe home. You are Mom and Dad. Following are first steps to capturing a cat's heart.

HOW TO MAKE A LOVE BOND continued

Respond any time he shows affection. Cats show love by circling your ankles, threading through your legs, kneading, touching with a paw, stretching front paws up against you, purring, blinking, jumping up to your level, licking you, rolling over to expose the belly, meowing, or touching noses...and sleeping next to you.

You can return his affection by kneading the back of his neck, saying his name, picking him up, running your cheek against his, or scratching his cheeks where he has scent glands so he has marked you with his yummy smell. Even in the middle of the night, at least acknowledge him briefly.

Greet and feed. Serve small meals several times a day. But don't set the food down without calling him by name, making eye contact or whistling for him.

Look him in the eye. When he walks in the room, catch his eye and say his name. Or pick him up and pet him. When you start looking him in the eye, he will do the same when he needs your attention. Once you start, there is no turning back. You will become your cat's overworked servant for life!

Get his attention with a cat whisper. Purse your lips and whisper *Pss Pss Pss* (like *psst* but without the t.) He will stand and stare as if a bird just flew into the room and listen intently to the next thing you say. But don't get too close to his face. That will be interpreted as hissing. Hissing is a long Sssssssss and means *Go away* in Feline. Pss Pss Pss is different than Sssssssss.

To a cat, smiling looks like a hissing face and can be misinterpreted, notes Tanya Traufield, Animal Care Supervisor at the Longmont, Colorado Humane Society.

Blink. When a cat blinks at you, he's saying "I trust you." Blinking is like sharing a hug.

Get down on his level. Cats are more relaxed when we're on the same physical plane. They're happiest if their basket is at our shoulder height, if they are sleeping next to us or we're on the floor with them. When standing, we are giants who could easily flatten them with one step.

Play...Then Play Some More

Can a cat toy change your life? YES! It's called Da Bird.

When Tanya told me, "Da bird is just magical," I was skeptical. I had used other "cat fishing" toys. But this one is different. *Da Bird is da bomb!* It's a wand with a spinning feather that's so life-like you'll swear a bird flew in the window. For hyper kitties, *Da Bird* is da cure. This is real bird hunting without the guilt and gore. The long, lightweight wand extends your range so you don't have to lean down to play and there are a choice of attachments for variety.

Play...Then Play Some More continued

Da Bird and their dangly mouse, *Cat Catcher,* are both made by hand in the U.S. If you want well-adjusted cats who don't need therapy, flip 'em *Da Bird.* To order, see CATALOG.

A ball feeder toy aka a puzzle feeder is fun for a fractious cat or one who needs more exercise, Tanya says. They are shaped like balls or eggs you can open and fill with

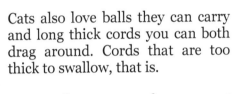

treats that fall out as kitty bats it around.

Cats also love balls they can carry and long thick cords you can both drag around. Cords that are too thick to swallow, that is.

Eventually, you can let your cat catch the toy.

A crackle tunnel/ tube is a great investment for under 20 dollars. The nylon fabric tubes have a stiff liner that crackles to the touch. (See previous page to see an example.)

When kitties go inside, you can tap the outside and send them into happy frenzy as they try to tap your hand. They love hiding inside, waiting to ambush someone or jumping out the hole in the top.

Empty cardboard boxes or paper grocery sacks are excellent cat toys that cost nothing. I think cats love to jump in boxes and sacks because they love to hunt hidden from sight. A favorite game in our house is the disappearing snake game. I open the bathroom door half way. Then I move one end of a terry cloth belt with my foot. The "snake" disappears mysteriously under the door with kitty paws in hot pursuit.

Catnip: Some get it, some don't. About 50 percent of cats respond to cat nip by getting very animated and rolling in it to cover their bodies with the scent. The effect wears off after a little while and then they get drowsy.

One of the 50% of cats who respond to cat nip.

Due to genetic differences, some cats don't respond. It can be a nice way to energize a quiet indoor cat and encourage play. They can become immune if used more than twice a week.

You can scatter catnip anywhere you wish to lure your cat...like on a scratching post for example.

Catmint and Catnip are different plants. Catmint is also attractive to cats and can have the same effects. You could plant either one in your outdoor Catio space allowing your cat free access. Catmint is invasive like a weed outdoors, so be careful where you plant. It requires little to no watering.

Cookie diving is a fun, bonding activity. You toss the cat treat (hereinafter referred to as a "cookie", **not a cookie for humans**), and the cat bounds off to chase it.

Play...Then Play Some More continued

combines hunting play with a reward for capture. You can hide "cookies" all over the house in a scavenger hunt when you're going away.

> *My cats have many hobbies:*
> *Hunting,*
> *pretending they are hunting,*
> *wishing they were hunting,*
> *and dreaming about hunting.*
>
> **Richard Kibbsgaard**

Give him a name he understands. Say his name often so he learns it. The best cat names have two syllables maximum and two contrasting vowels. Like *ah-oh, ee-ah, oh-ee, oo-ahh, ee- oh* and *oo- ee.*

Here are some examples of names based on this principle: Lucy, Ozzie, Chico, Moosie, Paco, Pokey, Rita, Johnny, Molly. Say them out loud and you'll hear what the cat hears: an obvious contrast in sound that's easy to distinguish.

Examples of names more difficult for a cat to understand (and harder for you to say!): McGregor, Tiffany, Ann, Ferguson, Sylvester, Ed. If it's one syllable, make it a strong sound like Ace, Bo, Maude, or the like.

Cookie diving is fun and delicious. Photo©Kerri Lee Smith

Chest hold. Feet are supported. Photo©Wikihow.com

How to Handle and Pet a Cat

Some cats get over stimulated and want to escape after a few minutes of handling. When a cat starts to wriggle, if you set him down he will usually come back around, rubbing against your legs. Here are ways to make them putty in your hands.

Chest hold: (pictured.) Holding kitty against your chest, your left palm supports back feet, your right arm crosses his back and supports under his armpits.

How to Handle and Pet a Cat continued

However you hold him, he'll feel better if his feet have support.

Over the shoulder hold: Just like it sounds. Rest front paws on your shoulder while supporting back legs in your left palm, and keep your right arm around his.

He'll love the high view that's not too confining. He can push off with back feet when he wants down so he won't feel trapped. *Again, when you feel him push off, set him down.*

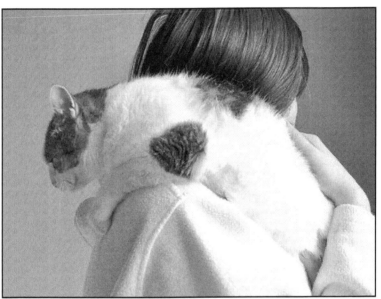

Over the shoulder hold. That's one cuddly calico!   Photo©Wikihow.com

Chin scratches: Scratch from throat toward mouth. Start gently massaging under chin and arm pits and gradually move to belly if he likes it. Don't pet his belly unless he enjoys it. Some do. Some don't.

Scratch his back just in front of his tail. He can't reach there to scratch himself.

Scratch between shoulder blades and knead the scruff. Remember? The scruff is that area on the back of the neck with loose skin.

Stroke the head with one index finger or three fingers max. Your whole hand is too heavy. Use fingers or thumbs on both hands to stroke the forehead where there are scent glands.

Stroke the sides of his face: Cup your hand and glide fingers from nose to cheeks and back to ears. Never the reverse. Remember, he has scent glands on his face on both sides. This marks your hands with his scent.

Stroke inside ears with index finger or pinky. *Caution, trim your nails first.* Graduate to whole ear massage especially behind ears on outside.

Massage gums: Some cats yes, some cats no...a good way to get them used to dental care handling.

Crazy Cat Lady Birthday Cake

Cat Calls

Cats meow at us but when they speak to each other, they chirp, trill, grunt or howl.

Runtie, the runt of the litter I raised, had about five different whiny meows of varying intensities to get my attention. He was a big drinker who preferred to drink from the bathtub faucet.

When he wanted me to turn on the faucet, he began by staring me down. Then he'd start to whine. If I didn't respond right away, it escalated to long, desperate meows: MAWWW, MAWWWW, like fingernails on a blackboard. So I taught him to signal he was thirsty by licking his lips.

First I asked, *Thirsty for water?* and turned on the faucet. Soon he learned the word *water*. Next I just said *water?* and licked my lips.

One day he caught my eye. I said, *water?* He answered me by licking his lips...proving that cats read our faces for cues. And they're smarter than they let on.

Photo©Sue Fockner

Secret Passwords / Special Handshakes

Try these secret words and moves to mesmerize your cats. They will be impressed when you speak fluent Feline.

Say *Mooshie Wooshie.* These words are calming, sweet talk. There's some-thing about the swishy sound cats like.

Technically it's *Spanglish.* In South America, I heard people call cats by saying *Michi, Michi (meechee)* instead of *Kitty, Kitty.* I tried it on my cats. They responded. Two repeated strong syllables. Perfect. Eventually it evolved into the magical *Mooshie Wooshie* mantra.

When you say *Mooshie Wooshie,* they blink and close their eyes. It may even put them to sleep.

Secret Passwords/ Special Handshakes continued

Chuffing: I learned this from a documentary; watching tigers communicate with each other. I tried it on my little ones...blowing out a *hoo hoo* breath...kind of like natural childbirth breaths. The cats looked at me as if I had just said the secret password and came running. Then they ran back and forth scent-marking me with their sides and face.

Chuffing will repel a cat if your faces are close. Blowing in a cat's face is like hissing. It means *go away*. There is a fine line between chuffing and blowing in his face. Blowing lightly over his body will usually get him rolling side to side, wanting to play.

Curiously, my cats have always responded to chuffing but I've tried this on other cats and it repels some of them. Perhaps it's because they have no bond with me.

When Molly was settling in, she was shy and hiding under the bed but when I chuffed at her, she'd come out, ready to play and interact. Experiment with chuffing and see how yours respond. Let me know.

Cat/cow stretch: This is a yoga move. I discovered its magic one day while exercising. You get down on all fours. First stretch your back up and round like a cat. Then stretch the opposite way, dropping your belly. That's the cat stretch. Then bring your back level and look to each side. That's the cow part.

My cats came running and each greeted me with a mouth touch, then ran back and forth under my body bridge repeatedly. Why does this move turn adult cats into ecstatic kittens? I think it's because I look like a Mom cat stretching.

Sniff their faces. This will often get you a nose touch. Watch cats greet each other. It starts as a sniff.

Sing their favorite song. What is their favorite song? Any tune with their name added to it. Cats love to hear their names and they do have music preferences. I could always lull Lucy to sleep by singing the Lucy Song. She preferred oldies and classic jazz and couldn't tolerate heavy metal.

Wrap them like a burrito. Cats seem to like being snugly wrapped. After a bath, or whenever kitty needs reassurance, wrap and gather him in a towel and breathe warm air on the top of his head.

Brush them. Most cats like brushing--especially if you start on the neck, behind the ears, under the chin, and then proceed to the back. Some cats act ticklish and can only tolerate it for a few minutes at a time especially on their tummies. Regular brushing prevents hairballs and keeps long-haired cats from getting dreadlocks

Shy Kitties

If kitty is hiding, he'll continue to hide unless you reach out. If he has good reason (see Cat Phobias) try to figure it out. A cat who has never bonded with a human or has been abused or punished, may withdraw or even attack.

Sadly, when it comes to this, he is often relinquished as incorrigible or left to remain in hiding with no human contact.

Here are tips for relaxing very shy or feral cats from Jenna Roger, the Longmont, Colorado Humane Society animal care supervisor. "We sit with them to introduce voice and scent recognition. We don't invade their space. Then we use tunnel tubes to get them to come out from their hiding space. Put food at the end of tunnel. We have encouraged them to leave their hiding spot but the tunnel makes them feel safe."

"Then we take away hiding spots, leaving one hiding bed only. We keep them in one small room. The other thing we've used with ferals is playing talk radio. They hear that conversational sound, know nothing bad is happening. When you sit with them they smell you, they hear you and they know nothing bad is going to happen."

After trying the above, try this: Visit the shy guy many times a day for a short session each time. Purse your lips and say *Pss, Pss, Pss* until he looks at you, then blink.

You want him to depend on you for food, so don't just plunk down a bowl and disappear. Set the food in front of you and wait until he comes to you. Even if he only eats a bit, take it away with you and come back fifteen minutes later, and go through the whole routine.

If he doesn't come out to eat, toss a treat in the space between you. Don't touch him until he emerges and hangs out. Then touch the back of his neck first.

Eventually, you will expand his world by bringing the food out further, offering a dangle toy or putting him in a room of his own, gradually enlarging his territory while handling him in non-threatening ways. He should come out when he sees there is nothing to fear.

Now you can initiate play, throw treats, and start to make a love bond, step by step. You may never be able to domesticate a feral cat but these tips will help relax a shy or fearful cat.

No whips, no spray bottles. Boots are optional and very chic.

TRAINING A CAT? What a concept!

Changing or even influencing a cat's behavior is a radical notion...even to many cat lovers. *Training* is actually a misnomer. A better term is *behavior modification*. It's the cats who train us.

A cat with good manners is easier to love. It's hard to enjoy living with a cat who has annoying and destructive habits or doesn't respond when you call or listen when you try to communicate. By setting a few boundaries and talking their language, we can live happily ever after with our tiny tigers.

TRAINING A CAT? What a concept! continued

Rule number one: Never hit or punish a cat. He can learn from your tone of voice and gentle, deliberate, repetitive actions. You want to exude authority to dominate him the same way his mother would.

Put away the spray bottles. Squirting them won't change behavior. It only teaches cats to run when they see the bottle. You want your cat to listen and learn your words and tone of voice. You want him to watch your face. You approve or disapprove using the same words with the same expectations and doing the same things every time. Every single time. *Consistency is what cats understand.* I've never used clickers though I know that some do and they have good results. You can't carry a clicker 24/7.

> *I had been told that the training procedure with cats was difficult. It's not. Mine had me trained in two days.*
> **Bill Dana**

Never punish for missing the box. It can make matters worse. There's always a good reason for litter mishaps. You can solve the problem by following the rules of proper litter box management. By keeping clean, getting the right box and enough of them and using the right litter, you can have good litter box Karma. More on this to come.

...or for jumping to a higher perch. He is just doing what his instincts tell him...finding a safe place. If you don't want him playing hockey with Grandma's Hummels, change his preference by offering him an alternative high perch. Keep moving him to the approved place. Distract and redirect. Put some catnip up there. Be consistent. Make it obvious...and stash your china in a closed cabinet.

We can only truly change a cat's *indoor* behavior. An outdoor cat's primal instincts take over once he steps outside. Outside, he becomes vulnerable. He becomes prey. Other cats are watching his every move, waiting to pounce on him if he trespasses. If he owns property in the country, he wants to hunt and oversee his territory and that takes precedence over most anything we mere mortals have to say. After you've given him time to complete his outdoor business, he should come home when you call. More on this topic coming up in *The Indoor/Outdoor Debate* chapter.

Hunting is your cat's most basic instinct. Hunting and yes, *killing*. If he goes outside, he'll try to catch anything that moves. It's his proudest accomplishment and though you may cringe at the very *thought* of him devouring some poor critter, he wants you to acknowledge him for bringing home the bacon. He wants to teach you to hunt, too, by saving you a tasty morsel, the way his mother taught him. If mother didn't teach him to hunt, he may be content to merely capture and manhandle his prey.

One of the saddest cats I've ever met was at a Colorado shelter. Tubbie (not his real name) had unknowingly infuriated his owners by having the audacity to catch a bird. So they called the humane society to pick him up in a field behind their house.

I bet Tubbie was punished before they banished him. He hung his head and shivered in my lap. He didn't respond or even make eye contact. He showed little interest in play. In a word, he seemed *depressed*. As soon as he was returned to his cage, he burrowed into a box at the back.

They could have put a bell on his collar. They might have kept him in a kennel. If his front claws had been trimmed, the bird may have escaped his clutches. Despite his "Sad Sack" personality, Tubbie was eventually adopted, hopefully to a more cat-friendly home.

I think cats get undeserved flack for killing birds. Birds also prey on their own kind and defend their nests. I witnessed a hawk attack and kill a dove in seconds from my kitchen window. I watched a blue jay dive-bomb my cat merely for innocently walking past its nest. My cat loped away, ducking and protesting loudly. If you do bell your cat, watch him because the bell could alert predators to his presence.

Be careful handling varmints. If you want to liberate  prey, be discrete and praise kitty first. If the plague is detected in your area, don't let them hunt. Cats pick up fleas from prey and fleas can carry plague. Beware of poisonous flea remedies made from Pyrethrins and Pyrethroids: insecticides typically used against fleas and ticks. If you live where fleas are a problem, before you buy flea killer over the counter, consult your vet. See the section at back: TOXINS/POISONS/DANGERS.

> *Cats are smarter than dogs. You can't get eight cats to pull a sled through the snow.* **Jeff Valdez**

Essential Skills for Cats

Here is my list of skills that every cat can learn with consistent, loving guidance. What's on your list?

Comes when you call. Knows what come here means, comes to a whistle or when called by name.

Understands NO and GET DOWN. Provide alternatives, though, if you forbid access to counters or certain high places. I visited a family who wouldn't even allow their cats on sofa backs. That wasn't fair because their kitties had no other alternative high perches.

Scratches only on approved posts or pads. More on scratching coming up in TROUBLESHOOTING.

Sleeps through the night...or at least doesn't wake me with claws or step on my face in the middle of the night. No fur-bearing mammals wrestling on the bed while I'm in it.

Doesn't jump on the counter. *Cat hair is not a popular condiment.*

Stays off the computer keyboard. *No, you can't have your own laptop.*

Doesn't attack human legs or hands. Even kittens can learn this. More on kittens to come

Doesn't rush toward an open door. Getting hit by a slamming door can be fatal to little ones. Or they may run out.

He can also accept and tolerate: riding in the carrier in the car (he should never ride loose in the car), pilling, having his teeth brushed, his paws handled and his claws trimmed.

The Thundershirt is a compression coat.

If your psycho kitty simply cannot relax or doesn't play well with others, you might try wrapping him in a *Thundershirt*, a jacket designed to gently hug a cat around the middle.

Based upon principles used in therapy for autistic humans, cats and dogs often relax even under stressful conditions when they feel the firm pressure of a compression jacket. Try it for car trips and going to the vet's.

Essential Skills for Cats continued

My cats ride better in the car if they can't see out the window. Cynthia B. has the world's most portable cat, the most well-travelled kitty I know. Her advice for calm cat co-pilots is "Start 'em young."

Try spraying your carrier with pheromone or calming sprays five minutes before you leave the house. I've seen dramatic results but not all cats may respond. It's worth a try.

Going to the vet's can be traumatic, but the more you go, the easier it gets.

If your kitty is vet phobic, you might try making some field trips to the clinic even when you don't have an appointment. Leave kitty in the carrier in the waiting room and then borrow an exam room and let kitty wander around with no other excitement going on. Then cruise around some before coming home to dinner.

Baths are optional but handy if your kitty ever gets muddy. For adult cats only. Small kittens shouldn't be bathed. They can get hypothermia. The water should be warm or it will be too much of a shock. Never spray a cat's head. Baths can be challenging if your cat is especially averse to water.

Cats can often be de-sensitized to water with patience and practice though it is easier to introduce them to showers when they're young. On really hot summer days, a tepid shower can be very refreshing for long-haired cats. They stay cooler for hours afterward!

The cat is the only animal to have succeeded in domesticating man. **Marcel Mauss**

This is my list of essential cat skills. What's on your list? When you choose behaviors to modify, take into account a cat's need to climb and explore up high.

Behavior Modification:
Using Voice and Hands

If you communicate with your cat in only three distinct voices he will understand you perfectly.

First, the **gentle, sweet voice** to express love and reinforce good behavior.

Second, the **angry voice, *used sparingly,*** when he's misbehaving.

Third, the **excited voice** to get his attention, call him to come or to follow.

Besides these, communicate with feline words: hissing, chuffing, *Pss Pss Pss* and *Mooshie Wooshie*.

Use angry voice only when he's breaking the rules. Stick to a limited list of naughty behaviors. You use only **two words** in your angry voice: NO and GET DOWN. Nothing else. Switch immediately to sweet voice when he complies and he will come to you for reassurance.

Make eye contact first. Firmly say "GET DOWN" (from wherever he shouldn't be) or "NO" don't scratch there, don't bite my hand, don't rush out the door etc. Just NO or GET DOWN. No other words. Loudly. Firmly. Just one time. You don't want to nag him. You want to make a single, non-negotiable statement.

With the side of your hand, *sweep him away* from a forbidden place while saying, GET DOWN. Then follow up with praise. It didn't take long for any of my cats to learn that jumping on counters made me sound angry. I only had to sweep them off the counter about four times before they decided it wasn't worth the drama. Because I *instantly* praised them, changing the tone of my voice to sweet, they knew I wasn't rejecting *them*, I just didn't like that *behavior*.

Some will take longer to respond, but be consistent and patient and your cats will learn. You can also try deterrents

Behavior Mod: Using Voice and Hands continued

such as sticky tape, aluminum foil or wetting the surface to assure compliance when you're not around.

Switch to the sweet, soft voice the minute kitty complies: *Good, good kitty. Such a smart boy.* For NO to work, you have to reward him with the sweet voice. Make it glaringly obvious that bad behavior has elicited the angry voice and compliance elicits the sweet one.

He does not like to be yelled at. When you switch to sweet voice, if he doesn't run toward you for positive reinforcement of his good behavior, seek him out and reward him.

Your cat may run to you for approval the very first time you teach him what NO or GET DOWN means and switch voices. Sometimes it takes a few times of switching voices and following up with affection until he learns. As soon as he runs to you for approval after getting told NO, you will know he gets it; you will see he wants to please you. It's proof that cats will alter their behavior to seek our approval.

Not scratching on his post? Distract and redirect. Say NO and move him immediately to the post and *praise him*. Put the post near where he wants to scratch. More solutions for scratching problems in the TROUBLE-SHOOTING section.

The third voice is a happy, excited tone for *Look, Cookies, Let's go, Where is...? Come here, Outside,* and to signal play time.

There is one more sound you can use to change behavior: **Hissing**. Hissing means: *Stop. Back off. Go away.* Use it sparingly.

Hissing is a dominating word that you can use to stop kitty from attacking with claws. Or stop a kitten from biting. It comes in handy when you want to teach a cat not to bother you when you are sleeping. Smiling can look like a hissy face to a cat.

Whistle and call him by name every time you feed and he will learn to come to a whistle and learn his name. You can also call out fancy beast (or whatever you wish) when you feed. Make your whistle sound like *You Hoo*, two tones, so he can understand it.

Shake the treat jar and yell *cookies* to teach the cookie word. It's a good way to get him to come when he doesn't want to.

This is the vocabulary I teach: *Cookies, Fancy Beast, GET DOWN, Come here, Outside, Let's go, Don't step on the 'puter, Jump, Look, NO, and Where is (name here)?* I teach their *names* and of course, they understand hissing, *Pss Pss Pss, Mooshie Wooshie* and chuffing. They have a vocabulary similar to that of a clever toddler.

To keep him from rushing toward an open door, every time I come or go, I call out: *LOOK OUT! Away from the door. OUTTA THE WAY.* I make it sound super scary.

I may extend my foot and catch kitty under the chin. During the training phase, I may drop a sack of groceries, making a loud, rolling crash to say: *Opening doors are dangerous.*

You can also use laser pointers to distract kitty from rushing a door. Not all cats will consistently follow the laser. If you use one, don't point it at their eyes.

Cats will sleep through the night if you feed them and play with them before bedtime. If they swat your face when you're sleeping, just hiss. They will learn not to wake you.

What greater gift than the love of a cat?
Charles Dickens

Your cat won't reject you because you ask him to get off the counter. On the contrary, when learns how to earn your praise, he will try to please you.

Optional Skills for Cats

Walking on a leash: To exercise indoor cats, you can take them for a stroll around your yard. Your neighbors will enjoy the show and your cat will have a fine adventure.

For this you need a harness or vest-type collar. Start inside letting him wander around wearing it. Then hook the leash and walk beside him with treats. If he lies down, set him up and throw a treat in front of him. Encourage him with your voice.

You can also use the end of the leash for him to chase like a carrot on a stick. Pretty soon he will feel comfortable walking and exploring in harness. Some cats eventually match their steps to yours but lead you around at first.

If he's an outdoor cat you're trying to convert to an indoor cat, he'll definitely want to lead you outdoors. If you walk daily, you'll notice he has a routine: He stops to sniff his peemail or leave his own mog blog; he scent marks the tree trunks with his paws, in order. He's marking territory. He'll be happier if you follow the same path each day.

High Five/Gimme Five is a cute trick. Cats who really love treats and attention can be trained to do tricks like high five, jump up, sit up, run agility obstacle courses, and more.

Lucy was a sucker for treats and learned High Five in about five sessions. I placed her paw in my palm and then gave her a treat, saying *Gimme Five*. Eventually, when I put out my paw, she patted it with hers to get the cookie. Note: not for declawed cats.

Jump (onto lap or chair, etc) is a handy skill when you want to pick up kitty without bending down. Pretty simple: Just point to the stool or chair and say JUMP and give the treat.

Cats who love food will sit up for a treat held just out of reach if you give him the treat afterward.

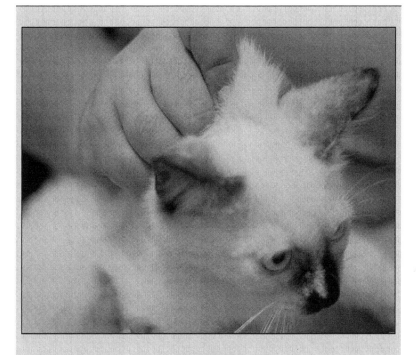

Scruffing

Sometimes we need to restrain a cat. Holding him down by force, though, only makes him defensive and uncooperative. Luckily, we have a little trick called *scruffing*.

Grasp him by the back of his neck, where the skin is loose. It's called the scruff. He has no feeling there. He instinctively goes limp, just as he did as a kitten when Mom carried him.

Adult cats don't like to be scruffed so use it for serious situations like giving medications or to stop a cat from biting.

See how the hand is supporting the cat's weight under his belly? You can lift a kitten by the scruff but an adult cat is too heavy to lift by the scruff.

Photo©Wikihow.com

Optional Skills for Cats continued

If you have a clever cat and want to do more training, I recommend Annie Bruce's website, *Cat Be Good*. You'll find the address in the Catalog at the end.

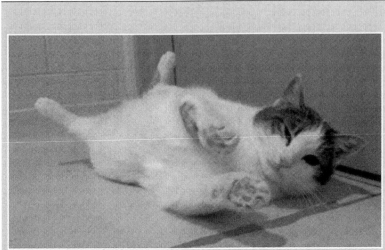

This is Bob V from a Toronto adoption facility...he's kneady!

Cat Scans

Kittens knead on Mom's tummy to bring out the milk. Later, it's a nostalgic re-enactment of happy nursing memories.

My friend, Richard Cargill, claims his cat saved his life by diagnosing his abdominal aneurysm. The cat was kneading Richard's abdomen when he felt the lump. He loves to tell how he was saved by an old-fashioned CAT scan!

CAT SKILLS for Mere Mortals

The first time you give a pill, trim toenails, or brush kitty's teeth is a good time to try a compression jacket, calming treats, or essences. You can read more about all of these in the upcoming TROUBLESHOOTING section.

Wrapping them in a towel immobilizes their paws while pilling but it's a bit cumbersome. As your cat gains trust and accepts your loving authority, you'll rarely need to scruff or restrain him. It just takes a little practice.

Trimming Toenails

Everyone benefits from giving kitty a peticure. Without those lethal needle points, he won't stick to your curtains like velcro. He won't draw blood when wrestling his pals or tapping you on the cheek. When he kneads your stomach, it won't feel like you're getting your navel pierced. Strictly outdoor cats, however, need their claws intact to climb and to defend themselves.

Start gradually and it won't be an epic struggle. If kitty resists having his paws touched, start handling them every day, gently massaging the pads until the claws extend. A good time to handle paws is when kitty is napping or waking up. When he readily lets you handle his tootsies and extend the claws, he will let you trim. You will use special scissors

Trimming Toenails continued

with rounded blades. You only trim the front four claws and side claw...*just the tip...* only about *1/8 inch of claw.* It doesn't hurt. A good place to trim is in the bathroom. Cats are more confident in a small space. *Don't cut where you see pink blood supply.* I saw some clippers at the store that supposedly warn you if you're too close to the quick. I haven't tried them so can't comment.

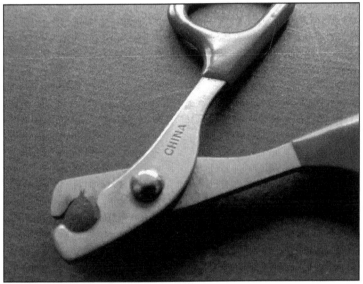

Cat's claw clippers have conical cutters.

Ready? Sit down on the throne (I'm assuming you are in the bathroom) and tuck kitty under your arm, supported on your lap. Pick up a paw and gently press it to extend the claws. Don't clamp down if he pulls away. Gently start over but keep him under your arm until you are successful *at least handling* one paw.

Don't end the session by letting kitty jump off your lap and run away. You want to end on a relaxed note so keep him on your lap after handling, brushing his face and neck for a reward. Then gently set him down. Make your first sessions short. You may decide not to trim the first several times. If you like, trim him while he's lying in his basket. Do whatever works and makes you both most comfortable.

You don't cut much. Just the sharp tip--about 1/8". If you see pink blood supply, don't cut there. There are many YouTube videos showing toenail trimming.

The first couple of times trim very shallowly. As your cat relaxes and you gain experience, you will take slightly more, always watching for the pink blood supply.

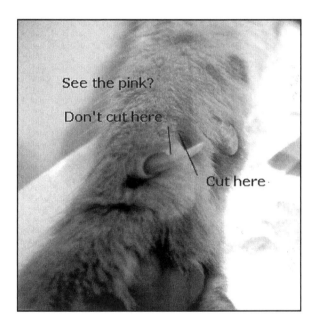

As your cat relaxes and you gain experience, you will take slightly more, always watching for the pink blood supply. I have never cut a nail to the quick in 18 years of trimming claws because I was conservative. So be careful, but don't overthink it.

Claws regenerate about every 10 days. Lucy and Runtie became so used to it, they went limp and purred as I trimmed. They often napped right through it. Wendy K.'s cats line up for claw trimming awaiting their tuna treat.

Giving Pills

Some cats are hard to bamboozle. They can detect the tiniest pill, the merest whiff of medication-even buried under a mountain of tuna. Learning to pill a cat is a proud and life-saving achievement that is easier with this technique.

First you coat the pill with cold butter or coconut oil so it slides down easily, tastes yummy and goes down whole. Set the coated tablet on a plate within reach. Get a little watered-down tuna juice or wet food treat ready for afterward or a syringe of water so the pill will be sure to slide straight to kitty's stomach.

Sit your cat down on your lap facing you.

With your left hand (if you are right handed) gently scruff him.

Pick up the pill with thumb and index finger. Insert your right middle finger in the side of his mouth where his whiskers end. There is a natural gap there. He will open. Drop the pill on his tongue as deep inside as you can.

Immediately close his mouth with your hands and massage his throat to help it down. *Then feed tuna water or wet food treat.* Praise him and give yourself a pat on the back.

It popped back out? Don't give up. Let's try it again.
1. **Butter it.**
2. **Scruff cat.**
3. **Grab pill and open side of mouth** with third finger.
4. **Insert pill** as deep as you can.
5. **Hold mouth closed** (optional depending on your bond)
6. **Massage throat** or blow into his nose (this is optional but may help him swallow.)

Finally, give water or wet food so the pill will slide down smoothly. Treats for everyone! Reward yourself with a treat and reward your cat with a nice neck and face brushing.

Homemade pill pockets will disguise the pill but not the taste. Some pills like Metronidazole taste horrid. They're large too. Here's how to pass one off as a sardine: Take a small fish oil gelatin capsule and cut one end off to pill size. Slide the pill inside it like a sleeve and fill it up with fish oil or butter. Coat the outside with butter and insert it the same way (you don't want him to chew it.)

Or use an emptied two-part gel cap...the transparent type. Or cover the pill with a **bit of firm cheese**. If you use pill pockets, just use a half and butter it The piece should be small enough to swallow and not big enough to chew.

Piller guns? I have two friends who love their pillers; syringe guns to inject the pill into the mouth. My method seems less invasive and less likely to cause an aversion. I had to pill Maisie three times a day for six weeks. She never objected after the first two times and became totally nonchalant toward the end. Whatever works.

*It doesn't **taste** like candy!*

Some meds can be compounded in liquid form in choice of flavorings. Consult your vet. Sometimes, because of the taste, cats will vomit liquids so pills are actually better tolerated. Liquid meds usually cost more. Dispense them from the side of the mouth, too. For hyperthyroid cats, there's a very effective topical medication that is rubbed into the skin on the inside of his ear. Photo© Jason Thorpe

Dental Care

If only we could teach cats to floss and brush! Some cats are lucky. They're genetically less prone to dental problems. But most cats older than two have some degree of gingivitis or tartar buildup in their mouths.

Left untreated, gingivitis can cause pain, tooth loss, and even systemic infection.

There are several, simple, preventive things you can do to care for their mouths: brushing, proper diet and certain treats and supplements. Your cat gnawing on a raw chicken neck is the closest thing to brushing his own teeth. If you feed raw chicken wings or necks, though, feed large chunks that can't be swallowed whole or cats may choke. For that reason, don't feed them unsupervised. Not recommended for small kittens.

Feed only large pieces of necks or wings. Photo©Hotash

Dry food keeps their teeth clean, right? I used to think so, too. Back then, I was feeding dry food exclusively and my cats still got gum disease. As I researched, pooling knowledge from many veterinarians, I found a consensus that busted this common myth. Here's why: Cats often swallow kibble whole, getting no abrasive benefit and dry food is usually higher in carbohydrates which are essentially *sugars*.

Prescription tartar-control dry food has larger pieces, designed to be chewed more thoroughly. But dry food may not be the best diet for your cat. We'll look at diet and how it affects your cat's health in the upcoming Feeding chapter.

I didn't spend much time pondering my cats' dental health until one day, during a routine exam, a vet probed Lucy's loose tooth and it came flying out! I had no idea my cat's mouth was as shaky as a house of cards! It was the beginning of my quest for better feline oral hygiene.

Yes, but I have my own brush. Photo©Kerri Lee Smith

Here's what I've observed from monitoring my cats' mouths: hold the gravy, hold the carbs, munching on mice cleans their teeth (or raw chicken necks or wings), cats who drink more water have better teeth and brushing really helps.

When I first introduced canned food along with the dry, I fed their favorites--anything "with gravy."

Dental Care continued

Their tartar doubled and their gums started bleeding. The gravy had to be the culprit; aka refined carbohydrate, aka *sugar,* sticking to their teeth.

When I stopped feeding food with gravy, corn, rice, glutens or flour, *their mouths improved dramatically almost overnight. Red gums to pink.* After their professional cleaning, I started brushing. It kept inflammation down. If I missed several days, I could see gum inflammation suddenly worsen.

Monitor the mouth. Joel Stone, DVM, says, people often don't bring their animals for professional care until the cat's breath is unbearable or kitty stops eating. By then, he says, the condition is serious. Cats are pretty stoic. You may not even know they have advanced gum disease unless you inspect their mouths.

Bad breath, red bleeding gums or loose teeth are signs of gum disease. Gum disease in the early stages can be controlled and treated, but it means an immediate trip to the vet. Your vet will anesthetize your cat and use ultrasound to clean under the gum line. If your cat is older, your vet will verify that his heart will tolerate anesthesia. All cats should be monitored with an EKG during the procedure. Dental extractions with full-body anesthesia and follow up X-rays tell the vet whether the tooth root is entirely removed.

Plaque is the soft, bacteria-rich layer that rapidly forms on the surface of the teeth if they are not brushed clean. Plaque turns into tartar when it calcifies.

Tartar is the hard coating, usually grey or yellow color that is resistant to removal by chewing or brushing. It's what your dentist scrapes off with metal tools. Tartar gives plaque a foothold.

You can keep your cats healthy *and save money* by learning how to brush their teeth.

Brushing will remove plaque and prevent tartar, but the only way to remove heavy coats of existing tartar is with professional cleaning. Scraping tartar with a dental tool won't cure active gingivitis because it won't clean underneath the gums. Only your vet can do that.

If kitty's gums are actively bleeding, he needs professional care. After you make an appointment, you can apply first aid to bleeding gums with *Oratene Enzymatic Antiseptic Gel* or chlorhexidine pet dental spray. The *Oratene Enzymatic Antiseptic Gel* has no flavor but chlorhexidine tastes bad. Dr. Jean Hofve also recommends making a natural dental spray for gingivitis made of decaffeinated green tea.

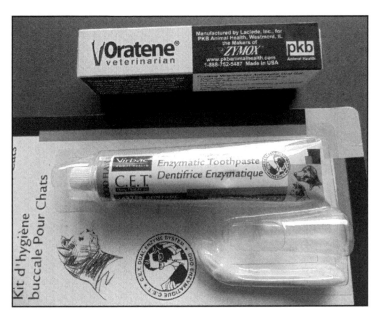

The best cat toothpaste I've found is C.E.T. brand. It is both antiseptic and fights plaque with enzymes. Most cats love the taste...even licking it off your fingers...a good way to get them used to the brush. There are two formulas and choice of flavors. The tartar control formula is slightly abrasive and comes in two flavors, but isn't quite as tasty.

You can use bare fingers to apply it, but keep to the outside and trim your nails.

Dental Care continued

You don't have to brush the inside of his mouth. His rough, sandpapery tongue keeps it clean enough.

The tartar control formula is slightly abrasive and comes in two flavors, but isn't quite as tasty. You can use your bare fingers to apply it, but keep fingers to the outside and trim your nails. You don't have to clean the inside of his mouth. His rough, sandpapery tongue keeps it clean enough.

The *C.E.T.* toothpaste comes in a kit with one small brush and one rubber brush. The rubber one is too big for a small cat's mouth. Your cat may prefer the brush. I love the *C.E.T.* brush. It's soft with long bristles that keep your fingers away from the chomp zone. Just swab each side back to front a few times and the fangs in front. You can reuse either brush over and over. Just rinse with hot water after use and replace when the bristles are floppy.

If you chicken out on brushing, you can rub the *C.E.T.* toothpaste or *Oratene Maintenance Gel* on teeth and gums daily. At least let them lick *C.E.T.* off your fingers for a start. *C.E.T.* and *Oratene* products are effective because they don't just disguise bad breath, they contain enzymes that actually fight plaque.

Cat chew toys or bones are a great idea for keeping teeth and gums healthy...*if your cats will chew them.* The best chew toys are raw chicken wing tips or cornish game hen necks (cooked bones are too brittle) in large enough pieces they can't swallow whole. I've tried loofa chew toys and mesh fabric toys. Some cats will chew the loofa, others show no interest in gnawing or noshing.

Beware of a toy that deteriorates with use.

What about dental treats? Most cats love *Feline Greenies*. They're meant to be abrasive to "help control tartar," according to the manufacturer, but make no claims to reduce plaque. Grains are a main ingredient, and again, to be effective they must chew treats, not swallow them whole.

The chlorophyll in them will improve breath but may disguise dental problems.

C.E.T brand dental treats, are antiseptic and clinically proven to control plaque and tartar. *C.E.T. Oral Hygiene Chews* (fish or poultry flavor) contain enzymes like the toothpaste. Freeze dried fish is the main ingredient with no grains or corn. The outer layer wrapping holds them together. They look like corks so cats bat them around like toys. If they don't consume them at first, they may develop a taste for them. Follow feeding instructions on the bag.

The chomp zone. Photo©Jason Thorpe

What about water additives? It depends on the flavor as cats can be finicky about water. Cats who eat a wet diet often don't drink much water.

Wysong makes a food additive called *Dentatreat* for cats and dogs made of cheese, pre and probiotics, minerals and other

Dental Care continued

natural ingredients to support dental health. If your kitty is a real tartar producer, there's a product called *Plaque Off,* a food additive made from seaweed. Because it's high in iodine, you can't feed it to hyperthyroid cats. If you have tried these, write me.

If you have a cat with chronic gingivitis, you may also try supplementing vitamins C and D. Ask your vet for dosages. Or switch to raw food. More on this in next section.

Attention cat food makers: I wish you'd add something to wet food for dental health such as enzymes or chunky, chewy bits that clean teeth...or something to alter the mouth PH to be less favorable to bacteria growth? Of course, any food additive would have to support whole health. *Please email me if you have any ideas.*

Conclusions

Monitor the mouth regularly to catch problems early. If you avoid gravy, grains, and flour, your cat will have a healthier mouth and need professional work less often. If your cat hunts and consumes whole prey or you feed chunky wet foods or chunks of raw meat with (small) bones intact, his teeth will stay cleaner. Feeding dental treats is only somewhat helpful.

Even makers of dental water additives, food additives and gels all recommend daily brushing in addition to their products. "Brushing is still the gold standard of dental care for cats," according to the spokeswoman for *Oratene* dental products. "Nothing replaces brushing."

This swill is an assault to my superior palate.
Photo©Viola, Viola's Visions

FEEDING:
Hold the kibble, hold the gravy

When we feed our families, we want to *nourish* them, not merely provide adequate calories and vitamins to keep them alive. We can nourish our pets with a variety of high quality proteins to help them live longer and feel better, too. Food is love and the right food is also good medicine.

Jean Hofve, DVM, who wrote "What Cats Should Eat," consulted with me on this very important issue of cat care. There's a summary at the end of the chapter if the following seems too technical. Don't miss: Human foods not safe for cats and Salmonella Debugged.

Here are the two most important facts about feeding cats: Cats must eat meat and they need taurine.

Cats need a high protein diet--protein from meat, animal organs, tissues and fat. You cannot have a healthy vegetarian cat by feeding only plant proteins. If you want to know the technical details. check out Messybeast.com.

Cats also need a daily supply of an amino acid called taurine either from food or supplements.

Wet or Dry?

Dry food is popular because it is convenient. It is cheaper... *at least on the front end.* After reading the most current research and from many years of personal experience, *I'm convinced that wet food is best for cats.*

Most veterinarians don't specialize in cat nutrition but some of them are dedicated to researching, studying and writing about it. Here are just a few of the veterinarians who are vocal promoters of feeding meat-based, wet diets only: Dr. Deborah Greco, Dr. Ron Hines, Dr. Elizabeth Hodgkins, Dr. Jean Hofve, Dr. Lisa Pierson, Dr. Mark Peterson, Dr. Andrea Tasi and Dr. Debra Zoran.

When I asked one of my own vets, Dr. Leah Hanley, her best tip for cat longevity, she answered in a split second: *"Feed wet food."* Following are several sound arguments for feeding wet food (canned, raw or homemade) to keep your fur buddies trimmer, happier and healthier for life.

Cats are carnivores. Cats have no biological need to consume carbohydrates. They utilize protein as energy. They have no amylase in their mouths; their digestive tract is shorter and less capable of processing starches*. Dry food is high-heat processed, made from lower quality sources, may contain allergens and/or contamination by molds or bacteria, and is higher in carbohydrates and lower in digestible meat-derived protein than wet food.

Prevent obesity to prevent Diabetes. Deborah Greco, DVM, a leading researcher in the field of feline diabetes, promotes the "Catkin's" diet, high in meat protein and low in carbs. "Feeding a cat dry food and refilling the bowl is the worst way to feed a cat. It promotes obesity," Greco says. "High levels of carbohydrate in dry food causes over-production of insulin, increased hunger and weight gain."

Obesity leads to diabetes. The results of a study done by Dr. Greco and Mark Peterson, DVM, showed that 68 percent of diabetic cats could be taken off insulin merely by changing to a high protein diet compared to only forty percent on a high fiber diet.**

Feeding dry food can cause chronic dehydration. Research on feline drinking behavior shows that even though cats fed dry foods do drink more often, they generally do not take in the same amount of water as cats who eat canned wet food.* Feeding strictly dry food can cause kidney disease because a cat may not get sufficient hydration over an extended time.

Wet food is about 70 percent water and is one way to ensure they're getting enough of that precious liquid.

If your cat is prone to urinary tract infections, consider feeding wet food. Dry food contributes to FLUTD (feline lower urinary tract disease) in two major ways: dehydration and alteration of pH.

Plant products (including the grains, fruits, and vegetables in dry food) tend to raise urine pH, and may predispose cats to lower urinary tract problems such as infections, crystals, stones, and blockages.

Wet foods usually contain more protein than dry, which helps keep urine pH low and less likely to cause crystals or stones.****

Feeding continued

Photo©Jason Thorpe

Dry kibble can cause chronic vomiting and intestinal problems. Cats tend to swallow it whole, often too quickly, then vomit. Vomiting leads to dehydration. Constipation can be caused by dehydration.

I had several cats who reacted with diarrhea and bloody stools if fed dry food with fiber content over three percent...symptoms of irritable bowel syndrome.

When I stopped feeding dry food, the same cats enjoyed *every type* of wet food with no gut-wrenching side effects. For years I cleaned up vomit...soggy piles of whole kibble.

When I started feeding wet food, there was no more daily vomiting. They devoured it- like having steak after a steady diet of cornflakes.

Mystery meat: How to decipher food labels. By law, all pet food labels must use certain terminology. "Meat byproducts" are what's left over once a carcass has been stripped of meat for human consumption. Byproducts include organs like lungs and kidneys, tissues and cartilage; perfectly good food *if they are fresh and not diseased.*

The worst quality ingredients in dry pet food are "meat meal", "meat and bone meal," "byproduct meal" (made from poultry by-products) "animal digest" and "animal fat." All these are made at rendering plants. Every type of carcass imaginable, including the four D's not considered fit for human consumption: dead, downed, diseased, and disabled animals, go into the pot to be cooked down and turned into "meal." Because some euthanized animals may be in the mix, the meal can be tainted with chemical residues as well.

The law reads: *Dead animals not suitable for human consumption must be denatured. Any carcasses or parts or products of animals which are not intended for use as human food shall prior to their being offered for sale or transportation, be denatured or otherwise identified as prescribed by regulations of the director to prevent their use as human food.*

In other words, in order to be sold or transported for pet food manufacture, all dead animals not fit for human consumption must be "denatured"; boiled down and rendered into "meal."

Better quality dry food contains *specifically named meat meals* such as chicken meal, salmon meal, turkey meal, and so on. They are also rendered but made specifically of leftovers from meat packing plants and not waste from a wide variety of outside sources as well. Better quality dry food is lower in carbs and higher in meat protein.

Best quality dry foods just name the meat like "chicken", "turkey" etc. and are not made from rendered ingredients.

To summarize, generic rendered ingredients are termed "meat meal" and made of more diverse waste and of questionable purity or quality compared to a specific named meat such as "chicken," "chicken meal," or "meat by-products." If it is "meal" it's rendered product.

Generally speaking, freshly slaughtered meat byproducts go into canned food and rendered products go into dry kibble.

Semi-moist cat treats are not considered wet food because they're made like dry food only with extra preservatives to keep them soft along with artificial colors.

Pet food ingredients on labels are listed in order by weight but the figures can be misleading. For example, chicken is the first ingredient by weight, but with the water removed, it is really a much smaller percentage. So, even a dry food with "high in meat protein " will actually have *less available protein as fed* because the percentage of protein was calculated before the water was removed. It's very confusing, I agree.

Many dry foods have up to 35 percent carbohydrate in them but most canned foods have less than 10 percent carbohydrate. To find the amount of carbs, look at the label under Guaranteed Analysis and deduct the values from 100%. The remainder should be the carbs.

Bottom line, *no dry food is as high in protein as canned or raw food* except for freeze dried or dehydrated food with meat as a primary ingredient or unless the canned food is high in non-meat fillers like fruits, vegetables and grains. One company sells kibble containing bits of freeze-dried raw food making it naturally higher in meat protein than other dry foods.

The very worst pet foods have a non-meat ingredient as the first item in the list.

Grain free doesn't always mean carb free. These are also carbohydrates: all fruits and vegetables, all grains, rice, potatoes, beans, peas, glutens, flours, corn, and soy. So "grain free" does not necessarily mean "carbohydrate free." I found no research to show that cats require or can metabolize and use as energy more than small amounts of carbohydrates**.

Eat prey, love. Rodents, rabbits and birds are true cat food; muscle, fat, bones, organs and water in the form of blood. There is less than 10 percent carbohydrate in prey animals. There's no rice, corn, flour, oatmeal, tomatoes, cranberries, blueberries, apples or other salad bar ingredients in the natural diet of a cat. Yet all of those and more are showing up in commercial cat foods.

"We have to build a better mouse," says Jean Hofve DVM. "A fat little mouse is the perfect diet for a cat." If your house or barn isn't infested, you can actually buy whole ground mouse carcass by the pound! Ironically, it costs more than Filet Mignon, which is one reason why my house panthers will not be indulged. But I will condone, and even *encourage them* to consume any rodents they find!

Besides carbs, here's a list of undesirable contents: "meat meal" (just that generic word,) "meat and bone meal" (the two lowest quality ingredients from a rendering plant), powdered cellulose (wood pulp) Ethoxyquin, Propylene Glycol, BHA, BHT, Benzoic Acid, Sodium Benzoate, Potassium Benzoate, Sodium Nitrite or Sodium Nitrate.

Other ingredients to avoid: BPA coatings inside cans, Carrageenan (may be irritating for cats suffering from Irritable Bowel Syndrome,) MSG, dyes and colorings and Menadione. You will read varying opinions about some of these but I think there is enough evidence to believe they are harmful, especially for a cat suffering from IBS. There are many other controversial ingredients depending upon whom you ask.

It's best to avoid any pet food made with ingredients from China. Contaminated wheat gluten imported from China caused the huge pet food recall of 2007. Some of the better

Feeding continued

products claim no ingredients imported from China. It would be impossible to prove in any product made from rendered ingredients in dry food, or made from imported chickens. Most vitamin supplements are made in China.

BARF is good: Biologically Appropriate Raw Food is similar to what a cat would get hunting live food. It has natural enzymes and nutrients not destroyed by cooking. I've read many accounts of cats being cured of inflammatory bowel disease when switched to raw diets.

Raw food with bony chunks to chew, will keep gums and teeth healthier, too. I've read accounts of cats with Stomatitis, a painful chronic gingivitis, being cured or alleviated when cats eat raw (but soft) food. I believe the enzymes in raw food improves mouth chemistry.

The raw and the cooked: You can make fresh BARF at home, freeze it, and it will cost less than good canned food if you get a grinder (if you are going to feed ground raw bone), follow a recipe to assure proper nutrition, and keep meticulously clean. The simplest way is to add *Alnutrin,* a complete powdered supplement, to meat and organs in the proportions they suggest. There are two formulas; one with eggshell calcium and one if you want to add your own bone. See CATALOG for details and free samples.

After handling raw meat, carefully wash your hands, countertops and anywhere you touch, to protect yourself from Salmonellosis and Listeria Monocytogenes. Feed small amounts your cat will finish quickly. Or you can cook it lightly to kill surface bacteria. Read Catinfo.org and Littlebigcat.com if you want a veterinarian's perspective on feeding raw food and Catcentric.org for feeding tips.

Raw bones are softer than cooked bones. Cooked bones are brittle. So if you make cat food cooked bones, you need to grind it. **Ask your vet if your cat can consume bones because they may not be safe for cats with kidney disease.** Fish and pork should never be fed raw.

Like most everyone, I was slow to adopt raw feeding. Now I am a believer. My cats have bloomed. They love chewing hunks of gizzard and wing tips. Their teeth and gums look great. Their coats glisten.

Photo©Jason Thorpe

I sought advice from a great website called Catcentric.org. And I found other experienced raw feeders on Facebook who shared their tips on transitioning, sourcing meats and recipes for home "brew". See the Catalog at the back for addresses or look on Facebook. Dr. Hofve recommends feeding lightly cooking raw food when first transitioning a cat with IBD to raw food, however.

You can buy frozen raw food and keep it frozen until feeding or buy freeze dried raw. Freeze dried raw food is only about 6 percent moisture. It can be fed dry or mixed with water. It isn't as susceptible to spoiling as frozen raw so it is safer to handle and store but it is still considered raw.

Freeze dried raw food is the most expensive food of all. It has the same disadvantage of dry food. It is dry.

Feeding continued

Dehydrated, powdered foods are neither raw nor fully cooked. They're supposed to feature the best aspects of raw foods because they're heated only to 160 degrees while being dried, yet you can store them on a shelf until feeding. You add water before feeding. They have no preservatives, so once you mix them, they shouldn't be left out more than 30 minutes, not unlike raw food.

"Made from human grade ingredients" is a new term some manufacturers use to market their products. By law, for a product to be considered edible for humans, all ingredients in the product must be human edible and the product must be manufactured and packed in a facility approved for human food production.

There is only one manufacturer I know of who won a court case to prove that they do use human grade ingredients in a human grade manufacturing facility and that is The Honest Kitchen (dehydrated foods.) Others may be using *human grade ingredients,* but they can't legally advertise it as such because the FDA requires them to manufacture in a plant *which also meets standards for human foods.*

If your cats have never eaten anything but dry food, you may have to persist in switching them to wet or raw diets.

But don't make 'em quit cold turkey. They can get fatty liver disease after just a few days without eating. One vet I know said her cat took three years to kick the dry habit! Topping wet food with some *Fortiflora* or *Advita* brand probiotics will make it taste more like the coating on dry food or you can top it with bits of crumbled kibble. And cats like their food room temperature. See websites in the CATALOG for more tips on transitioning.

Freezing meat for seventy-two hours kills parasites such as toxoplasmosis and worms. Most worms infest intestines and you won't find guts in commercial raw food.

Got milk? Cats like it but they're actually lactose intolerant.

Lactose-free milk or goat's milk are more easily digested.

Liver should make up no more than 10% of the diet. It's super high in vitamin A. Cod liver oil is also too high in vitamin A to give to cats.

Flaxseed, olive or canola oils are not metabolized as essential fatty acids. Fish oils are the best source of Omega 3s. Oils should be purified to remove mercury, PCBs and dioxins. You can overdose fish oils and vitamin A, say pet nutritionists. Give no more than 1,000 mgs per 10 lbs per day.

Photo source LOLdamn.com

Fish oils and vitamin E in measured doses are important additions to the cat diet because cats can't synthesize essential fatty acids.

Tuna contains high amounts of mercury and can cause kidney stones. Feeding tuna regularly can cause Steatitis aka

Feeding continued

Yellow Fat Disease. Canned tuna for humans is not a complete meal for cats. A little bit of low- sodium tuna juice mixed with water is a nice chaser with a pill, however.

©J.D. Crowe, jdcrowe@al.com

Salmonella Debugged!

Dry food and raw food have *both* been recalled for salmonella contamination. I was shocked to discover while searching the FDA website that their zero tolerance for salmonella contamination in pet foods is because *"...it can pose risks to human health when people who are "at-risk" (children, the elderly, and individuals with compromised immune systems) come into direct contact with contaminated pet food."*

In other words, recalls for salmonella are primarily *for protection of humans!* That's why you should wear gloves or wash your hands and all surfaces immediately after handling raw meat. Salmonella-contaminated food won't *necessarily* make your cat sick. It's more likely to make *you* sick.

Most table scraps have too much salt, fat or carbohydrates.

Homemade broth is the perfect kitty soup. Making unsalted chicken broth from boiling bones and cartilage is a healthy treat for kitties. Remove bones before serving.

Salmonellosis and Listeria *infections* are rare in cats.

Even healthy cats host the bacteria naturally. Salmonellosis can be hard to diagnose in cats for that reason. Their stomachs are very acidic and their digestive tracts much shorter than ours, so cats usually don't become ill from salmonella contaminated meat. It usually only causes illness if the animal has a weakened immune system due to disease, antibiotics, steroids or stress. Kittens are more susceptible. Kittens are more prone to digestive upsets in general.

Ironically, by law, *human grade raw meat* may contain an *allowable amount* of salmonella contamination since it is meant to be cooked before consuming which would destroy the bug. So we should be careful handling raw meat from *any* source. Raw pet food manufacturers are held to the zero-tolerance FDA policy against salmonella contamination

You could contract Salmonellosis from your cat if, say, he ate some contaminated food and you kissed him on the mouth or you handled his contaminated feces and put your hand in your mouth. It's usually not a fatal disease but more serious for anyone with a compromised immune system. Still, it is a good idea to disinfect your litter boxes when you change litter.

Again, I must stress, if your animals have diarrhea or vomiting for more than one day, consult your vet.

Wash hands and all surfaces after handling raw meat or serving it. Watch your animals for signs of illness. If you want to know what the FDA requires in pet food labeling, see my link in the CATALOG.

Feeding continued

No gravy. No rice. No flour. Aside from promoting plaque and tartar, gravy (made from flour), rice, wheat gluten, and corn will make sedentary cats fat. Some cats will slurp the gravy, leaving the nutritious chunks of "meat."

When you switch brands of dry food do it gradually, mixing old with the new to prevent diarrhea. Varying the flavors of wet food is a good idea to prevent cats from developing allergies.

Six reasons not to feed much fish: Most fish contains high levels of mercury, may cause urinary tract infections in susceptible cats, can be very low quality or contaminated by pesticides from fish farming and has inadequate levels of B vitamins. Fish can be addictive, making cats prefer it to anything else and it may cause older cats to develop hyperthyroidism. *Fish should never be fed raw.*

How much should you feed? Young kittens should eat as much as they want. Feed several times a day, so they don't gorge and vomit. They need kitten food for their first year.

Constantly refilling an empty bowl is overfeeding an adult cat. Older cats will eat about six ounces of wet food per day (preferably in three feedings) per six to eight pounds depending on age and activity level. Young or very active cats probably will eat more. If your *young* cat is hyperactive *and isn't overweight,* feed him when he asks.

Obesity is easier to prevent than cure. Dr. Zoran writes: "Obesity is incredibly difficult to reverse in the excessively obese adult cat, and, in many cases, requires lifelong management. Therefore, obesity prevention is essential."

In the same report on feline obesity she writes, "High-protein, low-carbohydrate, low-fat diets are ideal for weight loss in cats because they preserve muscle mass."***

Suddenly cutting calories can cause liver damage.

Weight loss has to happen slowly to be healthy. Dr. Hofve recommends no more than one percent body weight loss per month.

Consult your vet for a weight loss schedule for your chubby pal and increase his activity level in addition to changing his diet away from dry food.

You should monitor his weight daily if he's on a weight loss regimen and stick to a feeding schedule. If you have a diabetic cat, you may want to subscribe to an online support group. See CATALOG for the address.

No dog food for cats or vice versa. Feed your critters separately to be sure no one starves and everyone gets species-appropriate nutrition.

Photo source LOLdamn.com

To hear about pet food recalls first. If you subscribe to the FDA alert email service, you'll get a daily email regarding pet food recalls before they're announced elsewhere. See the link in the CATALOG section. Incidentally, dry pet foods are more likely than wet foods to be recalled.

Feeding continued

Feeding dry food in plastic bowls can cause zits.
Cats can get greasy chins as they eat kibble which can cause
feline acne; blackheads and big, gnarly whiteheads filled
with waxy sebum crud that can even get infected. Another
good reason to abandon kibble.

Fat Cat or Skinny Minnie?

According to the Society for Pet Obesity Prevention more
than half of American dogs and cats are overweight. Here's
their guide:

Healthy weight: Ribs are easily felt. Has tucked abdomen
with no sagging stomach. Waist can be seen when viewed
from above.

Overweight: You can't feel ribs under the fat. Sagging
stomach. You can grab a handful of fat. Broad, flat back. No
visible waist.

Summary

Cats need diets heavy in meat-protein, with sufficient
taurine.

"Meat meal," "meat and bone meal," "animal digest,"
"byproduct meal," or any generic "meal" is a boiled down,
rendered product made from lowest quality ingredients
more likely to be contaminated with undesirable chemical
residues. Rendered products are used almost exclusively in
dry food. Better quality dry foods contain specifically-named
meat ingredients. Best quality dry foods contain no "meal"
ingredients.

Most wet food, including canned, is higher in protein than
any dry food. Always transition slowly between dry foods to
prevent diarrhea. If transitioning from dry to wet, beware

that anorexia can cause liver damage. Don't overfeed. Reversing obesity can take years. Consult your vet for a weight loss strategy before putting an obese cat on a diet to avoid damage to his liver.

Nutrition affects dental health. Avoid canned food in gravy. Ask your vet if your cat has special dietary needs before feeding high protein, raw, or homemade food containing bones. Wash hands, utensils, counters, and plates after handling raw meat.

These are the basics of cat nutrition. Please consult the resources in the CATALOG for recipes and nutrition tips. *The Carnivore Connection to Nutrition in Cats* by Deborah Zoran DVM and *What Cats Should Eat* by Jean Hofve DVM are recommended reading.

Photo©Kerri Lee Smith

The Carnivore Connection to Nutrition in Cats by Debra L. Zoran DVM
**http://www.cabi.org/animalscience/news/13485
***excerpted from *Feline Nutrition: Understanding how to feed cats for obesity prevention and weight management,* published 2012 by Debra L. Zoran, DVM, PhD, DACVIM
****excerpted from *What Cats Should Eat* by Jean Hofve, DVM

Photo©Michelle Kelley

Have a drink...*PLEASE*

Here's another fun cat quirk: You can lead 'em to water but you can't make 'em drink. To keep them hydrated, try watering out of pitchers (some cats are afraid to get their paws wet so they avoid stepping near water), let them drink out of the faucet, water down their wet food (don't water dry food unless they will eat it immediately as it may spoil), serve watered down *sodium free* chicken broth and pet fountains.

Cats prefer fresh, flowing water and are drawn to a bubbling fountain. But be patient. They may ignore a fountain at first. *Thirsty Cat Fountains* are handmade in the U.S. and look like sculptures or art pottery. (see CATALOG to order.) The water bowl needs to be wider than their whiskers or they may be hesitant to put their head in it. I couldn't figure out why my cats boycotted the water bowl in my kitchen but drank from the water upstairs. Then I sniffed it. It was tainted...no doubt from bacteria passed from food bowls.

If you feed wet food exclusively, cats usually get enough water. Adding medicines or additives for dental health to water may repel cats. Yes, some kitties drink out of the toilet, so beware of toilet tank additives that could be harmful if consumed.

Dehydration can happen quickly and be fatal to cats. If your little guy is actively vomiting, has diarrhea, or stops eating or drinking, call your vet *immediately*. Your cat may need subcutaneous fluids to save his life.

Constant drinking can also signal a health problem such as diabetes. If your cat is drinking more than a few times a day or he's urinating often, consult your vet.

Photo©John Ginn

Hairballs: Retched Excess

The best colors for a cat lover's home decor include Bile Brown, Tabby Grey, or, if your cats hunt, a trendy taupe color called Moleskin. Regular brushing or combing helps

Hairball Cures continued

prevent hairballs. Most commercial hairball remedies are either high in fiber or petroleum jelly to help the hair pass. Petroleum jelly is safe but fiber may give kitty the runs. Here are some natural, food-based hairball cures:

Try adding some cooked pumpkin into the wet food or upping the fat content a bit with a little chicken fat or fish oil (but no more than 1,000 mgs a day per 10 pounds.)

Cat lovers also recommend serving a raw egg yolk...just the yolk...cats can't digest raw egg whites.

Grazing in the grass: Cats love to chew on oat grass, wheat grass or your lawn and it supposedly helps them to eliminate hairballs. You can buy oat or wheat grass seed and grow them this treat indoors.

> *Cats are not clean. They're covered in cat spit.*
> **John S. Nichols**

If your cat is vomiting daily, consult your vet. There's a difference between an *occasional* barfed hairball and chronically vomiting up food, liquid or just bubbles. If you constantly find piles of kibble vomit, try switching to wet food and feed several times daily.

Photo©Kerri Lee Smith

Photo©Kerri Lee Smith

TROUBLESHOOTING

Here is great advice from my humane society experts who see every conceivable cat behavior problem day in and day out: *If your cat is acting strangely, consult with your vet.*

One cat surrendered to them was infamous for biting...but only at the kitchen table. The mystery was eventually solved when the cat had a seizure. She had a neurological disorder. Litter box issues, too, can be caused by illness.

Litter. Boxes. *Oh the Drama!*

It's so discouraging when a cat boycotts the box. Usually, it's a simple fix, though. There's no need to get rid of the cat.

**Litter. Boxes. *Oh the Drama!* ** continued

If he's not using the box it's for one of the following reasons:

The box is dirty.

He doesn't like the box or litter. See next chapter.

He's sick. He has a urinary tract infection, urinary blockage or diarrhea. Male cats are especially prone to urinary blockages which are painful and life threatening. If your boy isn't peeing, it's an emergency.

Someone or something is threatening the area near the box.

Not enough boxes. You need at least one for each cat.

Box is too near his food.

He's declawed and it hurts to stand in litter.

He isn't neutered / she isn't spayed and is marking because of hormones.

Is he stressed? Or is he ill? A cat who suddenly stops using the box and has no other *new stresses* is most likely ill. If he's old, he could be senile. If you see blood in the box, call your vet immediately.

In that same shelter with Tubbie was a sweet little tuxedo cat, surrendered for not using the box. After a vet check, they found she had a urinary tract infection--no doubt the cause.

With antibiotics and proper litter box management, she would go back to perfect compliance. Meanwhile, she was stuck in a small cage with a horrible stigma haunting her, wearing the scarlet letter P, being passed over daily.

A cat who feels his territory has been invaded may purposely miss to mark with his scent. He's saying: "I deserve my own box and I'm not sharing with the new guy."

Once, when integrating a new cat and the incumbent together in the house for the first time, I noticed them dominating just one box. As soon as one used it, the other would run up and copycat.

I had three boxes--all separate locations. So why were they focusing on just one? *Were they were each marking it, claiming it as hers?* I wanted both to feel free to use *any box.* I didn't want *either one* to dominate *any box.* So, until they bonded, I immediately scooped each time after use. It worked. Neither one ever missed, sprayed or boycotted any of the boxes. They started out as enemies, but after the first week, they bonded and became as close as siblings. More on integrating a new cat to come.

Photo©Wikihow.com

At least one box for each. A bully cat may guard the litter box to keep others away. "Don't let one cat guard the box. Put the boxes in a place you can monitor. Every cat needs free access to a box," says Tanya of the Longmont Humane Society. Boxes should preferably be in a private or semi-private place. If you are going to change the location of a box, do it gradually, leaving a box in the old spot.

Litter. Boxes. *Oh the Drama!* continued

Kittens are especially loyal to their box location.

Keep it clean if you want them to use it. Scooping litter boxes allows you to monitor your cat's health via the contents and takes a few minutes each day. If you see bloody stools or diarrhea, take a sample for your vet to test. If you want to take a urine sample, you can use a small amount of white rice for litter and then strain the sample.

Beware of hooded boxes, top entry boxes, or tiny boxes: Your cat may be avoiding the box simply because of the design. Most cats wisely like to peek inside before diving into the toilet. Some cats want to jump out then cover while standing outside. Large kitties feel cramped in a hooded box and the hood traps dust for them to inhale. Some cats need tall sided boxes but open on top.

You can repurpose the box hoods. They make fun cat caves where cats can hide as you dangle a toy just out of reach.

A top entry box may even be already occupied: *Oh the horror!* Top entry boxes are harder to clean because you must open the lid.

Whatever box you use, make sure it is big enough and keep it away from his food and water.

Automatic litter boxes? I'm skeptical. We're walking on egg shells getting our cats to think inside the box. Why tempt fate with scary, new-fangled gadgets that may not even work?

On the other hand, Laurie M. and her fur kids are happy with their automatic Cat Genie. You hook it up to a water supply, it automatically rinses the tub of plastic pellet litter, filters then flushes the waste down a home plumbing drain. If you try it, she says, follow the manufacturer's instructions.

Some automatic-raking litter box sellers claim they only need to be emptied once a month. Seeing the size of the tray, and guessing the amount of waste produced per month, it doesn't make sense. And a strong smell would keep cats away.

There's a great website with an encyclopedia of litter boxes in the CATALOG section. If you try a new style box, I suggest you put out their familiar boxes as alternatives during the transition period to prevent accidents.

Declawed cats may avoid using the box because it hurts to stand in gravel. It can hurt their paws to cover.

Photo ©Wikihow.com

They need softer litter like shredded newspaper strips. If you care for one of these special kitties, see the CATALOG at back for a tip sheet on the unique issues facing declawed cats.

Kittens, declawed or arthritic cats need short, shallow boxes. A kitten's first box could be a tray one inch tall.

Spaying or neutering will reduce spraying, marking

Litter. Boxes. *Oh the Drama!* continued

by suitors, howling, caterwauling (I was hoping to get that word in here somewhere!) and, of course, unwanted litters of kittens taking up space in animal shelters.

Neutering also reduces cancer risk in both genders and roaming and aggression in tom cats. Unless you are breeding cats, there's no earthly reason not to spay or neuter.

At the end in FAQs is a link to low-cost neuter/spay clinics in your neighborhood. Your local animal shelter may also host a low cost spay/neuter day.

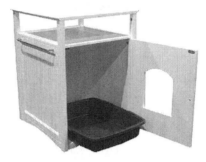

Merry Products Cat Washroom

If you see or smell urine, clean the spot immediately with *Nature's Miracle or Anti Icky Poo* which you can buy at pet stores. My friend, Suellen S., a cat shelter director, swears by *Anti Icky Poo*. It was developed to mask embalming odors! A strong vinegar solution will also work.

The cat will be drawn to pee in the same spot next time so it's important to get the smell off immediately. You could even move his box there. If you use a black light, you will discover any other areas. Plug in air fresheners for humans may actually deter your cats because of the strong perfume. Remember, their sense of smell is much keener than ours.

Some dogs will eat out of litter boxes! Dogs are silly. No self-respecting cat would eat a doody. So hide your box from the hound.

The Pick of the Litters

Preventing litter box boycotts may be a simple matter of switching litters. "The number one behavioral reason for cats to be punished, abandoned or surrendered to shelters is for not using the box. The proper litter can be the solution," says Gina Zaro of Precious Cat Products.

Their *Cat Attract* brand litter is designed to do just that. They sell an additive for that purpose too; a secret proprietary blend of herbs. Forty eight out of forty nine reviewers on a pet store website gave it the highest review (the other person gave it 4 out of 5.) Their *Kitten Attract* litter is fine ground clay which would probably also work well for declawed cats.

If cats shopped for litter they'd choose something absorbent to keep their dirty deeds secret with fine particles easy to fling and soft underfoot. It wouldn't stick to toes. They'd choose unscented litter because it doesn't smell overpowering and won't trigger asthma.

Shop shelves are literally littered with litters! How to choose? Each has pros and cons. There are several good options to please you *and* your cats.

Criteria for comparing litters are: dustiness, absorbency, odor control, adherence to paws (tracking), potential for allergens (for kitty and for you), ease of scooping, softness, clumping and potential hazards. The final factor is cost. *Litters are listed in order from cheapest to most expensive.*

Clay non-clumping litter is low in dust. It is least absorbent and heaviest so less is tracked out of the box and it doesn't stick to paws or fur.

Clay non-clumping litter is not effective for urine absorption or odor control and particles have sharp edges. If you use it alone, you will have to replace it often. It can be combined with clumping. Use about one third to two thirds.

Pick of the Litters continued

This mix saves money and still clumps but less sticks to paws or box. *Cheapest of the lot.*

Clay clumping litter varies in dustiness from almost dust free to very dusty depending on brand. Highly absorbent and covers odors. It can stick to wet paws. When cats clean their toes, they may ingest it. NOT for kittens who may try to eat it. Because it's meant to swell and form balls, the same can happen in their stomachs.

I don't like "extra hard clumping" types for those reasons and because it makes scooping more like hard rock mining. Some tracking but no allergens. *Low to medium priced.*

Blowing Smoke

Any inhaled silica or sodium bentonite dust (bentonite is the clumping agent in clumping clay litters) can be harmful to lungs, especially in asthmatic people or animals, but if you want to get technical, here's the fine print from the Sorptive Mineral Institute: *"Sodium Bentonite does contain small amounts of crystalline silica–the amount is generally between 0-10 percent. Crystalline silica, inhaled or airborne particles of respirable size, has been classified as a known human carcinogen, **but only in exposures from occupational sources.** The occupational sources referred to are applications that crush or fracture the crystalline silica grains such as sandblasting or grinding. The normal use of clumping clay cat litter is not an occupational exposure."*

Research done on cats both with and without respiratory disease* using clumping and non clumping clay litters is inconclusive, showing that while litter dust may exacerbate respiratory problems in cats, it may not be the cause. By law, if a product is deemed to be carcinogenic for humans in regular use, it should have a warning label. We should stay away from dusty litters of any kind to be safest.

Unscented, recycled newspaper litters are preferred for asthmatic cats according to a support group website. The brand we tested is not very absorbent, smelled strongly of ink the first time it got wet, and left black marks on paws. But we didn't test all brands. *Price is medium to high.*

Pine or cedar litters come as pellets or as clumping sawdust. Pellets are not dusty but less absorbent and less effective at controlling odor and don't clump. The pellets won't stick to cat paws but some of them come flying out of the box. Wood litter is recycled and isn't artificially scented. Not everyone will like the woody smell. The pellet type turns to sawdust with urine contact. Eventually you have to remove the sawdust or use a strainer box liner. At first, my cats only did number two in pine pellets but were eventually more forthcoming once it had broken down to sawdust.

Go online. Get a free bag!

The *Feline Pine Clumping* type is sawdust with mineral oil binder. It's almost dust-free and soft on paws with fair odor control but has a strong, woody odor, especially at first and makes weak clumps. Pine and cedar oils may irritate asthmatic cats. At Felinepine.com, you can get a rebate for a **free bag** of the clumping type. *Medium priced.*

Two other popular plant-based types are *Swheat brand* (wheat), *World's Best Cat Litter* brand (corn.)

Neither corn nor wheat types absorb as well or last as long as clay, in my experience. Both types stick to fur and paws and are tracked out of the box. Corn litter is somewhat dusty but the dust is supposedly not as damaging to lungs as crystalline silica or clay dust. Neither type clumps to make a hard ball.

Pick of the Litters continued

The corn clumps better than the wheat though I love the smell of the wheat. (One reviewer noted that cockroaches love it too.) The wheat is soft on paws but doesn't cover odor as well as some others. Wheat and corn litters are some of the most expensive. Some cats may try to consume corn litters. Corn litter is similar to a chicken feed called "Chick Starter" which is cheaper but contains vitamins, minerals and molasses so cats and kittens may want to eat it.

If your cats are constantly eating weird stuff, they may have a disease called **pica** which your vet can treat. Some cats even like to eat plastic bags!

I've read of aflatoxin mold in corn products, just to make the choice even more confusing. Most all corn grown in the U.S. is genetically modified. Wheat and corn types are biodegradable, but not for your veggie garden.

Ground walnut shell litter is low in dust with medium absorbency and odor control. It makes weak clumps. Fairly soft on paws but some tracking. I suspect this may stain white cats or cream-colored couches. *Price is on the high end.*

Silica (crystal) litters work by absorbing moisture and dehydrating solids. You scoop the solids and then stir the rest. When the crystals have absorbed to saturation point, they start to smell and you dump the whole contents. Important to note: There are two different kinds of silica crystals: synthetic *amorphous silica* gel and *crystalline silica.* The one that gets the bad rap for causing silicosis lung disease is the *crystalline* type.

Either way, the amount of dust may not be significant especially if your cat isn't a big digger. If you want the scoop on your litter see the CATALOG listing for litter ingredients. You only fill the box to one inch with crystals. I believe it also will lower the humidity level in your home and saturate much faster in a humid climate.

Silica crystals come in different sizes. Crystals don't adhere to coat or paws so silica is sold for long-haired cats. According to Gina, silica crystals don't support bacteria growth, so they can be used after surgery or during urinary tract or bacterial infections. It's also sold mixed with clay litter. *High priced* but you use less.

Sometimes art stinks. Photo©Ana Kelston

What do cat lovers prefer? One name stands out when polling cat lovers: *Dr. Elsey's Precious Cat Clumping Litter*. They say their clumping clay is 99.9 percent dust-free because they filter it before bagging. It's *much less* dusty than the comparables I've tried. The particles are finer so it is softer than some others and makes a firm ball.

It's more expensive among clumping clays, but less sticks to the waste so you discard less, somewhat offsetting the price difference.

Aside from the clumping clay made of 100 percent sodium bentonite, they sell several specialty litters and amorphous silica litter (the good kind). They have litters with chloro-phyll to mimic the outdoors, silica for long haired cats, for seniors, even hypoallergenic litters with herbal essences to

Pick of the Litters continued

suit cats with respiratory problems. Some types can only be ordered online. All are guaranteed. You can get a **full rebate** for your first bag and coupons if you go to their website: Preciouscat.com.

Go online. Get a free bag!

The easy way to clean a litter box is to tip it. All the solid wastes will separate. Every day or so add a little more litter. When it stinks, the litter is worn out so you toss it and clean the box. Keep it about three inches deep for clay or one inch for silica. Box liners are useless and will rip when you scoop or kitties dig. If a cat snags it with a claw, he may even develop an aversion to using the box.

My friend, Laurie G. has a huge herd of rescue cats. **She sprays her boxes with nonstick cooking spray** before filling so clods don't stick. Clever!

Follow your nose: If you can smell urine, your cat will need a gas mask since his sense of smell is 14 times more sensitive.

If you want your cats to use the box, you must scoop daily. Litters with heavy perfume or additives to achieve odor control, are not best for cats. No need to add baking soda to your cat boxes. Baking soda additives taste bitter when cats lick them off their fur. And soda is a dusty salt they shouldn't be consuming. *But an open box near the litter couldn't hurt.*

Pregnant women shouldn't handle cat feces because of the chance of contracting toxoplasmosis. Still, the chance is slim. Not all cats carry toxoplasmosis. If you have a bun in the oven, you can still enjoy your cats. Just keep your hands out of the used litter and avoid inhaling the dust. Or get your husband or kids to clean the box!

No litter should be flushed. It clogs pipes and pollutes groundwater. If you want to know about the ingredients in your litter see "Litter ingredients" in the CATALOG.

Good Litter Box Karma

If you are retraining a cat with bad habits, get some litter attract and add to the litter. Give your cats enough boxes, the style they like, in a quiet location filled with their favorite litter and scoop every day if you want good litter box Karma.

Most litters offer a money back guarantee or rebate.

Cats have the ultimate veto power. Before changing styles of box or type of litter, keep the old options open so the true connoisseurs can give it the acid test.

Wendy K.'s cats made their objections clear: *No wood chips please*, and very kindly used the bathtub instead.

Photo©Kate Tomlinson Flickr Creative Commons License

*From the Journal of the American Holistic Veterinary Medical Association — October 2001, Volume 20, Number 3, Page 13. "Detection of Silica Particles in Lung Wash Fluid from Cats With and Without Respiratory Disease."

Bringing Home a New Cat

When you bring home a new cat, your others may push him down, steal his lunch money, and refuse to play nice.

You can hush the *hiss*trionics and calm hostilities during the hazing process with a secret weapon called *pheromones*.

Pheromones are aromatherapy for cats; synthesized cat facial hormones that mimic scents they find reassuring...as if they have already marked an area with their own scent. This is a trick shelters use to calm cats being kept in close quarters. It can also help solve litter box issues and stress-caused scratching by calming cat anxiety. You won't detect any odor but it's joy juice for cats.

The most well-known is *Feliway* brand. For constant coverage, filling your house with good cat vibes, they sell plug-in diffusers that dispense a steady stream of the pheromone as well as spray bottles.

Sprays are good for short term uses. I like the diffusers when you need serious, ongoing help to soothe anxious cats who are constantly locking horns. I saw my fearful, timid newbie cat totally transformed after a few days.

Feliway's makers say to use their diffuser for a full month to be effective. Each diffuser covers 500 square feet. Once you see both cats facial marking an area, that will be a good sign that pheromone therapy is helping them.

I tried a pheromone collar by another maker but the collar was stiff, heavy plastic and my cat couldn't tolerate wearing it so I can't report on its efficacy.

I've used *NaturVet Quiet Moments Calming Room Spray* and seen amazing, instant results. I sprayed the car carrier and a cat I was adopting settled into the carrier without being asked and happily waited there with the door unzipped while we filled out paperwork.

You spray and wait five minutes for it to dry before exposing cats. You have to re-spray areas often. Not for use in kittens under three months. Feliway's product literature explains in detail how to solve specific issues.

Target the special space reserved for your new cat and common areas they will eventually share together. The following are tried and true techniques recommended by the humane society for integrating newly adopted cats.

Bringing Home a New Cat continued

When you first bring in a new cat, keep him in a small area alone, such as a bathroom, with his own litter box and toys for a few days. Visit him often to bond. Alone.

Next, switch places, letting them take turns having the run of the house. Put the incumbent in the bathroom and let the new one out. That way each can scent mark areas, and at least temporarily feel like the king of the castle.

If you have an outdoor enclosure, put the incumbent cat out there. You can also switch their bedding to expose each to the other's scent.

Plug in diffuser works 24/7.

After a few days, feed the cats on opposite sides of the door. They will be able to smell each other but still feel safe. The idea is that eating is pleasurable, so it creates a positive association for both. If either of them isn't eating well, don't try this. It can make a nervous cat anorexic.

After at least three days apart, you can integrate them for short times if they seem more relaxed, but only while supervising them.

The established one will usually dominate by hissing at the new guy to put him in his place. The new one will usually be more submissive...long enough for the old cat to accept him.

Keep the first meetings short so they don't get stressed. Eventually make the meetings longer. It could take a few weeks for them to stop fighting. Or longer.

Keep using your pheromone sprays or diffuser. If they're still acting like Snarky McSnark after a week together with no truce, you might need *Spirit Essences* brand liquid drops. There are formulas for nervous cats, bullies, scaredy cats, hyper cats and others. Because each cat is unique, you may have to try different things. *Bach Flower Rescue Remedies* are formulated to treat different emotional states in both humans and animals. You can purchase both types online (see CATALOG.)

Try cat calming treats. Most include B vitamins, L-Tryptophan, L- Theanine and herbs such as chamomile. I've gratefully fed them to hyper-active and hyper-thyroid cats and to my otherwise mellow cat who turned into a rabid wolverine in the car. Some work better than others.

For cats who just can't settle down at night even after an intense workout with *Da Bird*, there is a yummy treat called *NaturVet Quiet Moments* which contains some melatonin along with thiamine and L-Tryptophan and ginger. Just one treat magically transforms my party animal into a sleepy angel.

My vet warns against giving human tranquilizers or sleep drugs to cats.

To turn dueling devils into best buds, get them playing together. When they're mixing it up, distract them with a toy, drawing them both into the play.

When I adopted Molly, she didn't want to play ball on the new team. So I brought in a grasshopper from outside.

Suddenly, the two enemies reverted instantly into their primal roles, hunting together like family.

Jackson Galaxy has excellent YouTube videos on introducing new cats. He's the master at introducing cats.

If Your Current Cats Don't Get Along

You may have to reintroduce them. Try changing the environment by adding pheromones. Change how you relate to them to change how they relate to each other.

Give them equal time. Cats are jealous and possessive. They notice if you play favorites. Give them separate but equal facilities where you can be near both of them.

Give each one his own litter box away from the other so each can scent mark his space and dominate it. Feed them apart and don't ask them to share food bowls or sleeping quarters or locations. They may want their own toys that they don't have to share.

Jimmy and Mack mixing it up.   Photo©Kerri Lee Smith

Try the same techniques as for a newcomer: First separate them for a certain amount of time each day and during that time give each one your exclusive attention so neither witnesses you giving attention to their rival. Then switch their locations and keep them apart so that they are each in the other's space, but alone.

Give them a few high perches so they can escape each other. You can dangle *Da Bird* for them or their favorite toy. They may get caught up in the joy of play and declare a cease-fire.

From Enemies to BFF's

Hard to believe, but these two love bugs started out as bitter enemies.

I had done everything right when introducing them...without success. I was about to have a hissy fit myself after listening to them for an entire week.

Millie, the new one, finally broke the stalemate with a unique counter-offensive. She bowled her over, running straight into her full speed. Once was enough.

On the eighth day, finally at peace, they were tucked in their respective baskets, one on either side of my desk. Maisie tiptoed up to Millie and slowly and deliberately buried her nose in Millie's ear. It looked like a test of domination; to see if Millie would object or attack. Millie didn't move. She could no longer be considered a threat! Maisie returned to her basket with one last half-hearted hiss. It was the start of a beautiful friendship. Photo©Leslie Goodwin

Are Outsiders Bullying Your Indoor Cat?

Cats outside the house may be threatening your indoor cat, causing him to mark or spray. Following are four possible solutions.

Tip one: Mark your yard with used litter. Cats mark their territory with urine so you can sprinkle some all around the property line and especially near windows. You may have to do it several times a week at first to keep it fresh and then periodically afterward.

Tip two: Set a motion activated sprinkler called a *Scarecrow* or other motion-activated deterrent device near the windows to spray interlopers.

Tip three: Leash train your cat and when the coast is clear, walk him to each spot the intruders marked and let him mark it himself (granted this is going to work better with males.) It will do wonders for his mental health and establish his territory. A side benefit is deterring door-to-door salesmen.

As a last resort, ask your vet for drugs or get *Spirit Essences Safe Space* formula (see CATALOG.) My vet prescribed drugs for an anxious indoor cat who had been totally intimidated by cats threatening from outside.

Photo©Jason Thorpe

Some cats are just never going to get along despite our best efforts, say Jenna and Tanya. "Ultimately it is up to the cats. If you adopt from a shelter, most will allow you to return a cat if nothing works. Of course, try behavioral techniques first." They say that sometimes outdoor cats or larger numbers of cats get along better than when there are just two.

When you adopt from better shelters, the animals have been evaluated for how well they tolerate other cats, dogs, and children and given a "purrsonality" assessment. The best shelters even offer post adoption support to ease the integration process--another great reason to adopt!

Wendy K. has rescued many cats. She believes that rescue cats are quickest to adapt and get along with others.

Or you could skip the hazing process altogether by adopting a bonded pair from a shelter. Note to self: *Save for future reference, however it will increase cat inventory by two.*

Help! He's Shredding the Sofa!

Here are several, simple ways to save the sofa. No need to do anything drastic like declawing.

There is no reason to declaw a cat. Declawing is amputation. The first joint of each claw is literally chopped off. Declawing is horrific, cruel, unnecessary mutilation that can change a cat's personality forever for the worse. Just imagine how it might change your outlook if they amputated your fingertips! It can cause cats to stop using the litter box because of pain and to start biting and attacking. Declawing is banned in twenty two countries for good reason.

"Declawed cats usually have all kinds of behavior problems," Jenna explains. "And they're helpless outside. We had one that had been carried away by an owl. Somehow she escaped. There were huge slashes in her neck. Not surprisingly, she was very hostile and angry afterward."

Help! He's Shredding the Sofa continued

To add insult to injury, declawed cats usually develop bad arthritis. If you have a declawed cat, please refer to the catalog for a site with tips on caring for him.

Here's the good news: *Declawing is not necessary!* Besides providing a post or pad to scratch and training him to use it, you can trim his toenails, use nail caps, use adhesive tape called *Sticky Paws* or use pheromone treatments to end wanton scratching.

Sarah makes scratching posts that are works of art.
www.facebook.com/CatInTheBoxCreations

Cats need to scratch. They scratch to scent mark and to shed their claws. If you observe a cat outdoors, he will seek out trees, stretch up on two legs and drag his claws down the bark. He's scent marking it with his foot pads. So, a tree stump makes an excellent scratching post in your outdoor kennel.

Scratching is also a way for stressed cats to relax. If you have multiple cats, scratching sites are widespread, there are recent changes to the household or you see scratching near windows and doors. scratching is probably caused by anxiety. Review *Cat Phobias* if you think your cat is scratching to relieve stress and try pheromones, too.

You scratch my back, I'll scratch yours.
www.facebook.com/CatInTheBoxCreations

Some cats scratch standing up and some scratch on all fours. Finding out which your cat prefers will help you train him.

If he prefers floor level, you can make your own scratching pad from a regular 12 x 12 or larger ceramic floor tile and a woven straw placemat attached with hot glue.

Place posts or pads near where he is scratching illegally. If he prefers to scratch standing up, provide posts. Kitties get a

Help! He's Shredding the Sofa continued

nice back stretch on a vertical post so it's good to offer both posts and pads. Scratch it yourself to show him.

Put some catnip where you want him to scratch. When he scratches on the target, praise him.

I prefer rope coverings over carpeted posts. Since you don't want him to scratch carpet or upholstery, you don't want to train him to prefer those surfaces.

Whatever scratch pad you use, make sure it's heavy enough and stays in place.

When he starts scratching in the wrong place, pick him up and move him to the post or pad. When kitten Runtie was a young rogue, slashing his way through the house like Zorro, I moved him fifteen times in one day. It was a battle of wills, but after that day, he was forever bonded to his post.

Rub the inside of an orange peel anywhere you want to repel a cat. Or orange oil.

Another option is **Sticky Paws** brand adhesive strips with special two-sided tape you can stick to surfaces where you don't want your cat to scratch.

Nail caps are plastic caps without sharp tips you glue over actual claws. You cut them off periodically or replace them when they fall off. I have never used them. If you have to glue them on and cut them off, you may as well just trim the nails. I suspect nail caps may be a choking or swallowing hazard. Since cats are always grooming between their toes, what's to keep them from swallowing one of these caps or the dried adhesive?

Whether it's a bad habit or a stress reaction, during the training process, you can get slip covers and expendable area rugs. Rugs are replaceable. But you can't re-claw a declawed cat.

Photo©www.animalfriends.org.uk

Kittens are Truly Unruly

Kittens are adorable, cheeky little monkeys who spend a good portion of each day going berserk. You can expect them to climb the drapes, to hang from the chandeliers or take your ankle hostage. Unless they're asleep, young kittens usually don't want to cuddle as much as they want to use your fingers as a teething ring.

Like human siblings, kitten sibs alternate between joyful play and going for the jugular. Play fighting is how they learn to defend themselves.

Kittens are Truly Unruly continued

I don't recommend wrestling with them, but playing with kittens creates a bond and distracts them from being destructive. Begin handling their paws and mouths from the start. Give them short car trips in the carrier. You can even start leash training.

To discourage biting, *never play rough with your hands or feet.* Never tickle a kitten's tummy. If he latches onto you, stop dead still and say OW.

When he lets go, move your hand. If he bites again, say, OW, grab his scruff, and say, NO. Then turn your head away, stop playing, and walk away briefly.

When two kittens are wrestling and one gets too rough, the other will yelp to say "OUCH." And they'll both stop for a moment.

A pair beats one of a kind. Your kitten will grow up happier and better socialized if he has a feline partner-in-crime. A kitten about the same age is easier to introduce because some older cats don't have the patience or energy to tolerate kittens. You might as well have two little furry monsters trashing the house as one!

Introduce wet kitten food as soon as he is weaned. You can top it with a little milk replacer or goat's milk. If you feed a varied diet when he's young your kitten won't grow up to be a finicky eater...or maybe *less* finicky...when speaking of cats, it's all relative.

Kittens soon outgrow the silly phase. At least in theory. I have one who is a case of arrested development, still suffering from P.M.S.-perpetual motion syndrome-long after it could be excused as kitten behavior.

They mature quickly compared to human children. By their first birthday, they will be much quieter and more affectionate. Even cats who weren't cuddly as babies can become quite touchy-feely later on.

Feed kittens a varied diet so they don't grow up to be finicky.

Just when you run out of patience with the fuzzy little hooligans running amok, they grow out of it. With your help, they will grow up to be well-behaved with admirable skills having graduated from *Miss Leslie's Finishing School for Refined Felines.*

Kittens are Truly Unruly continued

It's unfair that loveable, mature cats are often overlooked at shelters while the little juvenile delinquents find homes. Older cats have survived some of the illnesses that strike only kittens.

Photo©Tom Godber Flickr Creative Commons License

Kitten Proofing

Kittens may swallow dangerous things such as loose buttons, yarn, string, dental floss or pills. Vets warn not to pull on a string sticking out of their mouths or coming out of their anus. If you suspect they've swallowed something suspicious, consider it an emergency.

To keep kittens from chewing on electrical cords by spraying cords with cheap, *scented* hairspray. Cats hate the taste and smell of it. Or use orange peel.

To protect houseplants you can cover the soil with fairly large rocks. Sharp edged stones are best. Sea shells work too. Or pine cones. Citrus oils applied to the edge of the planters may work too.

Some houseplants are poisonous. See the end for a complete list in the TOXINS/POISONS/DANGERS section.

Cleverly disguised, I stalk the wily foe.   Photo©Jason Thorpe

The Indoor/Outdoor Debate

Should you let them out? Keep them in? Or a little of both?

Obviously, if you keep your cats inside or enclosed in an outdoor *Catio*, they won't become a canapé for a coyote. Or have a run in with a car. They won't deflower your neighbor's garden, eat rat poison, or be taken or harassed by a cat-hater. That's a no-brainer.

On the other hand, they'll never know the joy of hunting live prey. They get less exercise. They command less territory. They may become bored. If they have no outdoor enclosure, they get no fresh air in winter. What are your options?

The Indoor/Outdoor Debate continued

Supervising them outdoors: Karen G. has reached a great compromise with her moggies. She accompanies them for a while each day in the backyard, keeping watch, letting them stalk lizards, and liberating the lizards afterward. This works because her cats can't jump the fence and don't try. It may not work for you.

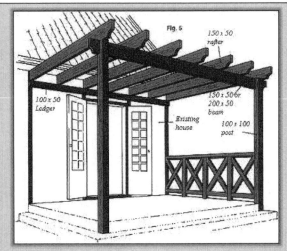

The Catio should be enclosed and cat proof.

Making the Case for a Catio

When Lucy strayed in, she was living rough. The first time she came indoors, she eyed the roof as if it might collapse on her. Attempts to keep her inside failed. She whined for weeks. When she gave birth to six kittens, I had to make hard choices. They wanted to follow mother outside. When she brought them mice and voles, they were hooked; delirious with hunting fever.

When a fox came into the yard, my heart stopped as I scooped kittens in my arms and the pasture horse ran it off. I taught them to fear cars by honking the horn every time they came near one. I worried constantly. One got hit by a car and didn't make it. One got hit and survived.

Isn't there a cat-proof fence? When I first tried to contain Lucy's rug rats, I researched all the fencing options.

My little monkeys could climb most anything. Runtie could jump a six-foot wood fence from a standstill. And in my country neighborhood, I must not only contain cats, I must fence out mobs of cranky, corn-fed raccoons and hungry gangs of coyotes.

Desperate times called for desperate measures.

I built an outdoor enclosure where they could be safe at night from Wile E. Coyote and the fiercest predators of all: motor vehicles.

I walked them on a leash. Runt would walk by my side, taking steps as I did. But Lucy reverted to the feral outside. I would hook her to a long leash and let her drag it as she wandered, only grabbing it if she tried to run. She soon flaunted her intellectual superiority by escaping the harness or waiting until my back was turned and bolting. She was too smart for me. I gave up trying to reprogram her.

I called them home every two hours and fed when they came home. When I whistled, Runtie would come running at a full gallop like Lassie coming to save Timmy from the well. Lucy would saunter in later...*most of the time.* There were nights I called until 2 a.m. probably because they had a mouse held hostage...or *they* were being held captive.

Letting my cats out took a huge toll on me, and I lost one of them. Every time they left the house, I knew I might never see them again. I only compromised because I had little choice. My current cats only go outside on a leash or in the outdoor Catio.

I felt sorry for my new captive cats, at first. Then in October, hordes of rodents were pillaging the garden. Millie caught 12 voles in one week...while on leash or in the Catio! She may hold the record for small game hunting in captivity.

The Indoor/Outdoor Debate continued

Some cat fences have a rounded top design to deter cats from climbing or broad jumping it. I'm not saying they would never work but I don't know of anyone who has installed a fence that contained a cat who was motivated to escape. Cats accustomed to wandering will climb or try to dig out. Neighborhood foxes, feral cats and raccoons could most likely climb it or topple it. Shock collar invisible fences are only for *dogs,* not cats.

I believe the only reason my semi-outdoor cats survived to old age was because of our outdoor Catio where they could spend evenings safely enclosed but still *al fresco.*

Molly relaxing on the Catio shelf. The top shelf is a curved visor for protection from the weather.

Every Feline of Uncommon Refinement craves his own outdoor pied-`a-terre where he can sunbathe, fantasize about frisky rodents, sneer at squirrels and torment grasshoppers--the ultimate cat toy!

The ideal outside cat kennel is enclosed on all four sides and sturdy enough to corral cats yet lock out coyotes, feral cats, dogs and raccoons and owls. Chain link fencing material works fine for all except tiny kittens who may be able to fit through the links.

The best "flooring" is natural grass. Cats love to chew, sniff and bed down in grass. There should be a covered perch safe from sun, rain and snow or a variety of perches at least four feet off the ground with access to the house, a good view and away from noisy threats like barking dogs, cars or motors.

Buddy Guy is dressed for the Canadian winter. Photo©JoanneWegiel
thecathouseinc.com

The Catio needs a full size access door you can lock if you suspect pranksters or forgetful kids might get in or leave the door open.

If the floor is natural grass, they may use it as a litter box, in which case, you need to poop scoop and water the grass to dilute the urine. If they prefer not to soil the grass, include a litter box out there.

A book shelf with sides makes a pretty good Catio shelf. The top shelf provides some shade and rain protection. A little cubby to hide in is also nice (in case someone scary comes by to visit).

Unless it has a roof, you need a tarp covering for shade in summer. Extra amenities for your Catio include climbing poles, water fountain, hammock, indoor trees, or tunnels.

The Indoor/Outdoor Debate continued

I made my Catio from a dog kennel kit. Then I bought a roll of chain link and a cross pole to span the top. It is 6' x 6' x 10'. It took a weekend to build from a kit.

You can buy cat doors to fit into a window. I removed one of the panes in an old sash window and built a flap door out of Plexiglas. Kitty kids can come into the house if I leave the flap open, or I can latch it shut.

The summer "cabin" is a smaller chain link cube with door that fits under a large tree.

You can also buy chain link dog kennel panels and join them with fence hardware...slightly more expensive than a kit but less labor. You could throw one together in a few hours with a helper. If you Google *Catio*, you will see many designs and plans for your own customized cat camp.

Think strong and completely enclosed. Some kitties will try to dig out or climb out at first!

A feral tom cat, the size of a bobcat and with the same coloring, once jumped to the top of my Catio and climbed to the second story window via the roof giving my cats and I a mighty fright.

Your outdoor cats need updated rabies vaccinations. Bats, raccoons, skunks and coyotes can spread rabies with a bite. Bats can sneak into your outdoor enclosure too.

Speaking of lawns, I wish they'd stop making pesticides or "weed and feed" for lawns. Not only do cats and dogs get it on their paws, lick it off and consume poison, it stays in the soil, contaminates the ground water and it may be killing bees who feed on treated weeds.

To make your garden a poop-free zone cover the soil with chicken wire or pieces of metal wire fencing. Cats won't tinkle where they can't cover.

A handsome senior cat from an adoption website.

MY BUDDY is OLD

How can this be the kitten you raised? Suddenly he walks with a rickety, stiff gait, slower to get up and unable to jump to his usual perch with ease. He needs a step stool next to the bed. He needs softer padding in his basket. You bring a litter box upstairs to save him the hike. Maybe even a shallower one.

Even though he never had a sick day in his life, your old buddy may one day stop eating, develop a chronic infection or seem depressed and lethargic. He may have trouble chewing because of tooth loss and his eyes cloud over with a bluish haze.

MY BUDDY is OLD continued

Sadly, we will never be in sync as we age. Our cats are aging at least four years for each one of ours (they age quickest in their first two years.) As they age, we may lose track of time passing. Sixteen years, the average life span, is never long enough.

Elderly cats may suddenly gain or lose weight due to thyroid conditions, diabetes or other diseases. Weighing them regularly is important. Over the age of ten, vets say they need blood work yearly even with no symptoms. Blood tests show their true state of health. I've included support group websites in the CATALOG for three common ailments of old age: hyper-thyroidism, diabetes and chronic renal failure. Members have a wealth of practical knowledge in managing a chronic condition and offer friendship and support during a challenging time.

Cats age better if they're at optimal weight; neither emaciated nor obese. Most old cats need glucosamine supplements for their stiff joints. As cats age they lose kidney function. It's crucial to keep them hydrated to flush their kidneys, so you may have to water down their wet food and feed small amounts more often. It won't hurt to increase taurine as well.

There haven't been many studies on how to increase longevity in cats. One study done on cats older than ten on the affect of certain supplements on longevity showed:

Senior cats fed a diet containing supplemental antioxidants vitamin E and beta carotene, dried chicory root (prebiotic), and a blend of Omega 3 and Omega 6 fatty acids lived significantly longer than cats fed a standard nutritionally complete feline diet. Positive trends for decreased incidence of thyroid and gastrointestinal pathologies suggest that the nutrient blend may provide some protection against certain disease states that may contribute to their increased longevity.*

Bringing home a new cat may be too stressful for an aging cat. Old guys may be more fearful and not up to meeting someone new.

In old age, it's essential that anorexia or vomiting be noted and diagnosed as soon as possible. In the last two years of Runtie and Lucy's lives, after age fifteen, they had several episodes when they stopped eating and drinking for no apparent reason. We gave them meds, subcutaneous fluids, and high-calorie vitamin gel.

Sister Lynn with dear Runtie. He crossed the bridge in 2013.
Photo©Leslie Goodwin

During those two years, they went from being near death to completely normal several times, so it was easy to be in denial when they made the ultimate turn for the worse.

At that point I was glad I had a relationship with a house call vet who also specialized in home euthanasia. House calls and phone calls saved us the stress of going to the clinic. I found it comforting to have fast access to drugs to treat pain and other symptoms.

Very old or terminally ill kitties need palliative care to treat symptoms and alleviate discomfort. The ideal vet is honest and open and helps you make sense of the sudden or confusing changes in your cat.

*Excerpted from Effect of Nutritional Interventions on Longevity of Senior Cats. Carolyn Cupp, DVM, Clementine Jean-Philippe, DVM, Wendell W. Kerr, MS, Avinash R. Patil, BVSc, PhD and Gerardo Perez-Camargo, PhD, MRCVS

Nine Lives are Never Enough

After living a decade or more with a special cat, it's hard to imagine life apart. Then the day comes, despite our best care and intentions, when it's obvious our buddy is fading. Yet after years of nursing and nurturing, when we find ourselves in the moment, it can be painful to let go.

Our cat buddies approach the end with dignity and stoicism that inspires and in an ironic way, consoles us. Their instincts tell them to hide away, to be alone in their time. My friend, Trudy, who studies Buddhism, once told me that animals have no attachment to the future. They live only in the present.

This is nature's perfect plan. It is some consolation to remember that by outliving our pets, we needn't worry any longer about leaving them behind. Just as they come into our lives by a happy twist of fate, changing our lives forever, they can leave it in the same surprising way. We humans are the only ones doomed to anguish over it. Animals can't choose to prolong their lives by extreme measures. Even if they could, why would they? They have no fear of the future.

By confronting our loss in order to end their suffering, we achieve a bond greater than any other. We become partners for all time.

> *There are two means of refuge from the miseries of life: music and cats.*
> **Albert Schweitzer**

Most cat lovers with a terminally ill cat wrestle with the same question: *How will I know when it is time to let him go?*

In my experience, the answer is to listen to your cat. Your cat will let you know when it is time. In one way or another, your buddy will try to tell you.

Grieving

After losing a loved one, we're haunted by a terrifying thought: *I'll never love or be loved as deeply again.* We are burdened with regrets--baggage we lug along on our grief trip: *Why did he have to get sick? Why didn't I see it coming? Why couldn't I have saved him? Why did I wait so long to put him down? Should I have waited longer?*

We can invent dozens of *woulda, coulda, shouldas* that serve only as guides for the future but do nothing to change the past. Somehow, we forget the many happy years together and focus on a few difficult days, weeks, or months.

Loss can leave us feeling numb, paralyzed, broken beyond repair...yet deep inside flickers a pilot light of hope. Sadness is one color in a whole rainbow of emotions that are our privilege and burden as mere humans.

The challenge after loss is to banish regrets, reject fearful thoughts and stow that oppressive cargo. Relief comes from believing that *love is perennial. The supply is never-ending. Love grows where it is planted and thrives where it is nurtured.*

Fear not. When you are ready, the Cat God will be waiting to match you again with the perfect feline friend. You can never replace a loved one...but you can carry on a beautiful tradition with your new loved ones.

To love at all is to be vulnerable. Love anything and your heart will certainly be wrung and possibly broken.

*If you want to make sure of keeping it intact, you must give your heart to no one, not even to an animal. Wrap it carefully round with hobbies and little luxuries; avoid all entanglements; lock it up safe in the casket or coffin of your selfishness. But in that casket—safe, dark, motionless, airless—it will change. It will not be broken; it will become unbreakable, impenetrable, irredeemable. **C.S. Lewis***

Grieving continued

Is someone else at home grieving? Twice, I've witness-ed cats grieving the loss of their cat companions. Was I imagining it? Were cats actually *grieving?*

Since then, I've found hundreds of stories of cats visibly mourning a loss by howling, ceasing to eat, looking for the lost one or by withdrawing.

The ASPCA Companion Animal Mourning Project in 1996 studied grieving in animals. The majority, 67% of animals in the study, exhibited behavioral changes at the loss of an animal companion.

Lucy at age 16 with a bad haircut. Photo© Leslie Goodwin

Grief is complicated when you have to share it. The animal survivors may be distant just when you need a cuddle. You may resent the surviving cat because he's too needy or acting out, not eating, or vocalizing. The survivor may search for the lost one, making your loss feel even sharper.

Opinions vary, but most writers say that showing the body will not necessarily help him to understand. They recom-mend leaving the house intact for a while, not moving the lost kitty's bed or removing his scent right away to ease the transition.

Cats thrive on routine, so reinforcing regular habits and rituals will help you both recover.

Your first reaction may be to ease your pain by replacing the lost one. But the new kitty may suffer by comparison because you haven't had time to let go, to come to the acceptance stage of grief.

Confronting a new cat soon after a loss may be very stressful for your other buddies. Your other kitties may need medication to get them back to eating normally. Time is the only cure for your broken hearts.

I tried to wait, to follow this official advice. So, when Runtie and Lucy had used their ninth lives, I went to volunteer at the humane society. I could do foster care and not make a commitment.

When the time comes, how will I ever choose my next two, I wondered, passing cage after cage of the hopeful homeless. *Impossible.* But one face stood out from the crowd of needy faces; one little waif who was the spitting image of my recently departed, Lucy.

I was just going to say *Hello;* a short visit as an emotionally detached volunteer, but Maisie climbed to my neck and clung on like a Velcro scarf. She had clearly chosen me. I was *catstruck.*

Out of 350 cats available at shelters near me, I met with four and brought two home. They were two perfect opposites who eventually meshed perfectly together.

I don't think it was luck or intention. I think a force much greater than us is at work. Our fate is in the hands of the Cat God.

Cats continually teach us an invaluable lesson: *Control is an illusion.* You don't pick them, they choose you. The next time I went to the shelter, shopping *intentionally,* desperately seeking a "replacement," none of the cats picked me. I thought I was ready, but the cats knew better.

Our fate is not in our hands. A greater force is at work.

I had doubts when Molly chose me. She was a shelter veteran, landing there twice in only eight months. In only two years, she had lived in at least four homes. She was fearful, withdrawn and peed outside the box. I was reminded that all relationships, feline *and* human, are a work in progress, requiring patience and love to succeed...and in this case, a hefty dose of cat phero- mones!

It has been challenging but very rewarding to foster her trans- formation, helping her to shed her unhappy past and claim her rightful home.

Molly, the shelter veteran

At the shelters, they say many adopters overlook the black cats. I used to pass them over too. Now, some of my best friends are black cats.

Adopting a cat is a little like getting married after only one date. You're pledging to love a total stranger; a frightened, needy stranger with a mysterious or dark past; and always carrying emotional baggage.

You have to believe that whoever you find, or *whoever finds you*, was divinely chosen to be yours. When you make that leap of faith and surrender yourself without expectations, you may be shocked at the intensity of your bond and the healing power of your love.

Mickie and Minnie. Photo©Sue Fockner

Guardian Angels in Fur Coats

Cats have an uncanny knack for finding a savior in their hour of greatest need...and an extrasensory ability to recognize someone who also needs saving.

My neighbors were grief-stricken when they lost their beloved 18 year old tabby. One morning, a week later, they heard an orphaned feral kitten meowing at their door. Was it a coincidence when a scrawny pregnant cat strayed in just as my friend's plans to adopt a baby fell through, giving her six furry "children" to raise? Or were these guardian angel cats on a mission?

I think cats are excellent judges of character even though we sometimes fail to live up to their expectations. They try to train us despite our lack of cat sense and instincts. We have lousy hunting skills. They bring us prey, but we never learn to catch anything.

Guardian Angels in Fur Coats continued

We can bridge the gap between us and make a love bond by understanding our cats' primal instincts and learning their language. By tweaking the environment a bit to suit them, we can help cats feel welcome, safe and confident.

We can ask them to modify their behavior to please us by setting boundaries and consistently communicating in ways they understand. If we dominate them in a loving way and consistently meet their needs, we can win their trust and earn their devotion.

> *When I am feeling low, all I have to do is watch my cats and my courage returns.* **Charles Bukowski**

The ideal relationship? According to WebMD, stroking a cat lowers your blood pressure. Studies show that cat lovers are less likely to suffer from strokes and heart attacks. Babies raised with cats are significantly less likely to develop asthma as they get older. Cats are perfect companions for disabled, homebound or retired people because kitties don't need to be walked or eliminate outdoors.

A cat will stay by your side when you are ill, listen when you complain and look worried when you cry. Unlike human children, you don't have to spend a fortune buying cats designer clothes or worry they won't come home for Thanksgiving. You don't have to buy them diamonds or annuities. They won't cheat on you by seeing others behind your back, (even if they may temporarily suck up to the sitter while you are away!)

Living with perfectly imperfect cats teaches humans to be more humane.

While we fuss and fret and take ourselves too seriously, cats remind us to play more, act silly, take more naps, and savor even the simplest of pleasures.

Our cats are guardian angels in fur coats, the sound and vibration of their purring a happy mantra spreading deep contentment as vital and as reassuring as a baby's heartbeat.

Ex voto retablo painting by Selva Prieto Salazar

Every life should have nine cats.
Anonymous

Coming up TOXINS/POISONS/DANGERS, FAQ's and CATALOG of WEB RESOURCES.

Colby Procyk reads to a shelter kitty. Photo © Katie Procyk

Book Buddies

At the Animal Rescue League of Berk's County, PA, kids read to cats and everyone wins. Children learn to read with non-judgmental tutors while making friends with lonely kitties. The cats hang on every word, mesmerized by the rhythmic sound of the children's voices, according to shelter super-visors.

The Book Buddies Program was implemented by Program Coordinator, Kristi Rodriguez. Her son, Sean, who's ten, struggled with reading at school so she brought him in to read to the cats. He loved it and asked to come back. So she invited other children to come and read. Since the program officially began in August 2013, Sean has made remarkable improvement in his reading. According to studies performed by researchers at Tufts University:

Human-animal interaction can make the learning process more comfortable and enjoyable for children. Autistic children who were put in contact with an animal demonstrated increased use of language and had improved social interactions while with the animal. They showed sustained focus and maintained a higher state of awareness, as well as improved attitudes toward school.

Everyone knows, school is more fun when cats come to class!

About the Author

Leslie Goodwin is a longtime cat lover and advocate. She was a working journalist, is an award-winning fiction writer and she wrote a bestselling Kindle book: ANTIQUE or Shabby Chic? *Appraise & Sell Like a Pro!*

In CAT SKILLS she shares advice from veterinarians, animal behavior experts and cat lovers along with hundreds of hours of research to offer a comprehensive guide to caring for cats with information about products, feeding, training and even helpful internet sites. She's a volunteer moderator on the F.I.P. Yahoo Support Group website. She lives with two rescued kitties who are constantly trying to teach her new tricks. Photo©Ted Martinez

The greatness of a nation can be judged by the way its animals are treated.
Mahatma Gandhi

Next: TOXINS/POISONS/DANGERS

TOXINS / POISONS / DANGERS

Please call your veterinarian immediately if your cat has been hit by a car or has any of these symptoms: diarrhea, persistent vomiting, not eating or drinking, not urinating, is abnormally lethargic, talking or crying constantly, urinating out of the box or grooming excessively, trouble breathing, coughing, bloody stools or urine or bleeding from the mouth. Do not give pets human pain killers.

If you suspect your cat has ingested something poisonous, call 888-426-4335 (24/7 a fee may be charged) or your veterinarian during office hours.

Babies left in hot cars can die and the same is true of cats and dogs.

Common hazards found around the house include antifreeze (ethylene glycol or even propylene glycol which is marketed as pet friendly-kitties like the taste and can consume it,) curtain cords (hanging hazard,) rodent poison, dental floss (easily swallowed), electrical shocks and warm car engines (outdoor kitties climb in for warmth and then get killed when the car is started.) Also toxic: Some flea killers (made of pyrethrins or pyrethroids), human medications (especially pain relievers,) mousetraps, new carpet (it off-gasses dangerous chemicals,) rubber bands, strings, tea tree oil, tinsel, thread, and treated toilet water.

These are harmful when stuck to paws or consumed: Road salt/de-icing salt, pesticides, weed killers, fertilizers, bleach and household cleansers, pyrethrins insecticide and homemade play dough. Mosquito repellant products with DEET are not safe for cats or dogs.

Marijuana is poison to dogs and cats. According to the Animal Poison Control Center, Marijuana is poisonous to pets. Marijuana, or THC, affects receptors in the brain that alter normal neuro-transmitter function. Dogs and cats can be poisoned by marijuana from second hand smoke, from  direct ingestion of marijuana or baked foods (e.g., pot brownies, pot butter, etc.) In dogs and cats poisoned by marijuana, clinical signs can be seen within three hours and include severe depression, walking as if drunk, lethargy, coma, low heart rate, low blood pressure, respiratory depression, dilated pupils, hyper-activity, vocalization and seizures. Vomiting is often seen with dogs.

If your animal has eaten marijuana, call your veterinarian or Pet Poison Helpline immediately for life-saving treatment and advice.

Some house plants *can be* poisonous to cats. This is from the ASPCA website. Don't panic if you have some of these plants around. Your cat may not touch them and for them to be dangerous, most need to be consumed.

TOXINS/POISONS/DANGERS continued

Flowers and plants that cause rashes/dermatitis:
Cactus, Chrysanthemums, Ficus, Poison Ivy, Poison Oak, Pothos Ivy, Primrose, Schefflera and Sumac.

These can cause upset stomachs/vomiting, diarrhea, and gas if eaten:
Amaryllis, Aster, Baby's Breath (Gyposphila), Boxwood, Calla Lily, Carnation, Chrysanthemums, Clematis, Cyclamen, Daffodil, Jonquil, English Ivy, Gladiolas, Holly, Hyacinth, Hydrangea, Kalanchoe, Peony, Morning Glory, Poinsettia, Pothos Ivy, Schefflera and Tulips.

No Mistletoe for Mittens. Photo©Tommy Hemmert Olesen

Flowers and plants that can cause death if eaten:
Agapanthus, Azalea (in large amounts), Cyclamen, Delphinium, Dumb Cane (Dieffenbachia), Foxglove, Jimson Weed, Lantana, Larkspur, Mistletoe, Oleander, Rhododendron, Sago Palms and Easter Lilies.

Lucy does yoga. Photo© Viola, Viola's Visions, Flickr Creative Commons

FAQs Frequently Asked Questions

How can I find a great vet? Ask your friends. The best vets won't do declawing. The ideal vet tries to answer questions over the phone, responds quickly in an emergency, and listens well. Your vet should be honest, kind and loving toward you and your cats and be willing to try anything to cure them.

What kind of worms do cats get? Outdoor cats who hunt and eat prey usually get tapeworms by ingesting fleas carried by rodents. Tapeworms aren't deadly but can cause vomiting, sap a cat's strength or interfere with eating. You can buy Praziquantel over the counter or have your vet recommend treatment. There are several ways to diagnose tapeworms. You may find little white segments on the cat's fur near the anus or in his bed. They look like flat rice grains. Kitty may pass or regurgitate one or continually vomit with nothing coming forth. A fecal test is another way to diagnose tapeworms.

Heartworms in cats are contracted from mosquito bites. Ask your vet if heartworms are a problem in your area.

FAQ's continued

How could my cat contract rabies? Rabies is spread by the bite of an infected animal like a bat, raccoon, skunk, fox, or coyote. Rodents and squirrels rarely carry rabies.

Can I get rabies from my cat? You could get rabies if your cat has rabies and bites you. If an unvaccinated cat has been bitten by a rabid carrier (like a bat, for instance) and is suspected of having rabies, the cat should be quarantined to prevent his spreading it. In fact, most cities require it.

Can I get worms from my cat? Probably not- unless you consume his feces or his fleas.

What diseases can cats pass to humans? The most common are rabies, toxoplasmosis, ringworm, roundworm (you would have to ingest the larvae,) and cat scratch fever (*Bartonellosis*, which not all cats carry, incidentally and is not usually fatal...just causes flu-like symptoms.) Wash your hands after handling puppies, kittens cat feces. Don't let them poop in the vegetable garden and don't let any animal lick your wounds. If you get scratched, wash the scratch with soap and water right away.

How can I clean cat hair off furniture or clothes? Dampen a sponge and rub it across the hairy surface. Magic.

Will cats hunt more if you feed them less? House cats hunt mostly for fun, not necessarily because of hunger. Cats who hunt and eat prey still need supplemental food and regular worming.

Photo source Catbearding.com

Why do cats like being in the bathroom? They feel safe in a small space where they can see who else is near.

How can I keep kittens from chewing electrical cords? Spray cords with cheap, scented hairspray or orange oil.

How can I give my indoor cats more exercise? With interactive play. Flip 'em *Da Bird*. Or set up an obstacle course and teach your cat to run it, walk your cat on a leash outdoors or try a puzzle feeder. They even have specially designed cat treadmills.

I found a feral cat. Should I trap it and take it to the animal shelter? No. Feral cats are usually not tame enough to be adoptable, so it may be euthanized at the shelter. Call a local feral cat rescue group. They do TNR; trap, neuter, release and vaccinate and feed feral cats to maintain colonies in place without overpopulation.

My kitten has diarrhea. What should I do? This is common among kittens under one year. Your vet can do a fecal test for parasites and bacteria. If the test is clean, try adding probiotics, (Advita and Fortiflora are two brand names) for a month and a little cooked pumpkin or squash to the wet food until things firm up. Many vets recommend a diet of wet food for loose stools.

Can I train my cat to use the toilet? You could but it's asking for trouble. It goes against a cat's natural instincts not to cover his waste. Cats who use the toilet may eventually start having accidents. What if someone forgets and closes the lid? What if he falls in? He'll never go there again...and he has no alternative.

How do you take a cat's temperature? What is normal? Use a well- greased plastic rectal thermometer. Scruffing recommended. Normal temp is 101 to 102.5.

Should I trim my cat's whiskers? No. They're his feelers...how he gauges his ability to fit through a space. My friend, Liz, says if you find one it's good luck.

Do cats get sunburned? It is not common but yes, short haired white cats with pink skin can get sunburned noses, ear tips, or bellies where the hair is short. They need shade outdoors. Human sunscreens can be harmful to pets who lick them. There are some pet sunscreens. It's safest to limit your white cat's time in the sun.

Don't hate me because I'm beautiful. Photo© Magnus Brath

A cat pours his body like water on the floor.
It is restful just to see him.
William Lyons Phelps

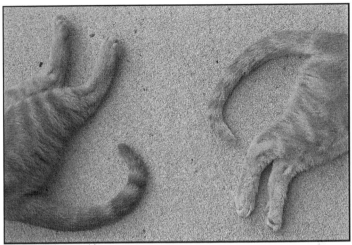

Photo©Kerri Lee Smith

CATALOG

Here are the websites mentioned. The support group sites are invaluable if your cat has a chronic illness. The rest are technically sound sites written by experts. I'm sure there are some I've missed. Email me your favorites.

Alnutrin *supplement for home made food. Free samples.*
knowwhatyoufeed.com
Bach flower essences: *bachflowerpets.com*
BPA coating in cat food cans list:
unitedcats.com/en/forum/280/46008/pet-food-alert-which-pet-foods-have-bpa-free-cans
Cat agility training: *monkeysee.com/play/16750-cat-agility-training*
Cat lore: *messybeast.com*
Cat supplies /Canada: *theCathouseInc.com*
Chronic renal failure support group:
groups.yahoo.com/neo/groups/tanyas-ckd-support/info
Communicable diseases cats/humans:
cdc.gov/healthypets/animals/cats.htm

CRF website: *Many health tips even if your cat doesn't have CRF. AKA Tanya's site: felinecrf.org*
Da Bird and Cat Catcher interactive toys: *Order from Go-Cat.com*
Declawed cats special care:
thecatsite.com/a/declawing-post-surgery-care-and-complications
Diabetes support group:
groups.yahoo.com/neo/groups/Felinediabetes/info
Feeding, FDA guide to what's on food labels:
> *fda.gov/AnimalVeterinary/Products/AnimalFoodF eeds/PetFood/default.htm*
> *fda.gov/animalveterinary/resourcesforyou/ucm04 7113.htm*
> *petfood.aafco.org/DefinitionofFoodDrugs.aspx*

Feeding, making cat food at home, vet tips:
Catinfo.org, Catcentric.org and Feline nutrition.org, knowhatyoufeed.com
Feeding, vet tips: *Littlebigcat.com*
Feliway pheromones: *www.feliway.com/us/Frequently-Asked-Questions*
Forums/advice from cat lovers: *Catsite.org*
Fun reading: *Catster.com*
Health info: *Winn Feline Foundation*
Merck Manual Online:
merckmanuals.com/pethealth/cat_disorders_and_disease s.html
Hyperthyroid cats support group:
groups.yahoo.com/neo/groups/feline-hyperT/info
Litter box reviews: *Thebestlitterbox.com*
Litter ingredients: *US Dept. of Health and Human Services householdproducts.nlm.nih.gov/*
Low cost spay and neuter near you: *aspca.org/pet-care/spayneuter*
Peeing outside the box:
vet.cornell.edu/fhc/health_resources/brochure_housesoilin g.cfm

Pet food recalls by email:

www.fda.gov/AboutFDA/ContactFDA/StayInformed/GetE mailUpdates/ucm2005606.htm

Spirit Essences and behavior tips: *Jacksongalaxy.com*

Training Tips: *www.catbegood.com*

Feel free to email tips: Incatrader@comcast.net. If you are a manufacturer and would like me to evaluate or review a product for a future edition, contact me. You can find me on Facebook at www.facebook/Leslie Goodwin, writer. Please spread the word and leave me a five star review on Amazon if you enjoyed this book! And check out my other book, **ANTIQUE *or Shabby Chic? Appraise & Sell Like a Pro.***

Thank you for adopting. Thank you for rescuing or volunteering at your local shelter.

I will gladly sell the paperback to animal shelters at a greatly reduced rate. If you would like to include my book in your adoption packets or sell in your gift stores, please write me at incatrader@comcast.net.

Maisie and Millie.   Photo©Leslie Goodwin

For Maisie
and all the F.I.P. Angels

F.I.P. is a deadly disease that mostly strikes kittens. To help cure it we raised funds with a crowdfunding campaign.

These friends donated to help cure F.I.P.: Krista Ann, Christine Keith, Stacey Jeffries, Laurie Dameron, Ted Martinez, Melanie Meilleur, Chrystina Goin, Lola Toney, Jacqueline Sheridan, Miranda Brennan, Kelly Richards Kapella, Kim Jesson, Paula Campbell, Susie Viel Powers, Lynn Goodwin, Charlene Laxton and Jesus Lopez. Thank you so much.

To learn more, see my video on Youtube: Angels in Fur Coats.

Also by Leslie Goodwin:

What is it? What's it worth? How do you sell it?

A bestselling book with secrets to help you appraise or sell your antiques and heirlooms.

Available online in eBook or paperback.

Leslie Goodwin

Made in the USA
Middletown, DE
25 July 2016